THE

ACACIA

STRATEGY

Revised
Edition

Bobby William Austin

Austin Rudd Press
Washington, DC

The Acacia Strategy is a series of five issue papers designed to suggest an innovative set of themes and narratives to guide new educational thinking and policy directions.

Austin Rudd Press

ISBN 978-1-0987073-7-8

Includes bibliographical references

Printed in the United States of America 2012

DEDICATION

This volume would not have been possible without the vision and support of Dr. N. Joyce Payne, founder of the Thurgood Marshall College Fund (TMCF). It has been her guiding wisdom, insight and encouragement that has brought this work to fruition, and established the TMCF as a major voice in American education. This work is dedicated to her as one of our foremost education pioneers.

This volume is also dedicated to Dr. Carolyn Rudd for unwavering belief and support in this book. Without her determination and support we would not have been able to put these ideas into print.

Special thanks...Ming Lowe, of CRP, Inc., is the man whom upon I depend. Thanks once again.

Bobby William Austin

August 2012

SPONSOR

This report was made possible by the generous support of the Thurgood Marshall College Fund and CRP, Inc.

Disclaimer

The ideas and concepts developed in this report are those of the author and do not necessarily reflect those of the Thurgood Marshall College Fund.

TABLE OF CONTENTS

FOREWORD

Historically Black Colleges and Universities (HBCUs) have been significantly under-utilized as national assets in advancing public education, particularly educational reform, a pillar of President Obama Administration's domestic policy agenda. HBCUs play a critical role in higher education systems and are poised to make even greater contributions to addressing the varied challenges facing our nation's public education infrastructure. HBCUs, for example, can assume leadership roles in serving as catalysts for innovation in America's education, strengthening education and workforce training, and reducing the racial disparity in STEM (science, technology, engineering and mathematics) careers, etc. Fulfilling the promise of HBCUs by enhancing innovation and by building on their cultural and historical legacies are the principal thematic underpinnings of *The Acacia Strategy*, an expository treatise designed to guide and inform policymakers as well as education administrators and practitioners.

As the President and Chief Executive Officer (CEO) of CRP, Incorporated (CRP), a nationally-recognized management consulting and professional services firm with strong ties to the U.S. Department of Education and the HBCU community, and a product of a HBCU, I am pleased to present *The Acacia Strategy*. This publication features a series of five issue papers that call for a stronger investment in and commitment to innovations and sustainability at HBCUs; both of which are critical for the long-term viability of these institutional resources. *The Acacia Strategy*, a seminal addition to the literature on educational policy, proposes an innovative sustainability plan for African American public higher education in the 21st century. *The Acacia Strategy* was written by Bobby Austin, PhD, a senior associate at CRP, with funding from the Thurgood Marshall College Fund. Dr. Austin also serves as the managing director of CRP's online think tank, an innovative community or laboratory of scholars and thought leaders engaged in intellectual inquiry, incisive analysis, and public discourse on educational policy. Dr. Austin has held senior, executive-level positions at the WK Kellogg Foundation, the University of the District of Columbia, and the Village Foundation, where he served as the founding president. He was the founding editor of the *Urban League Review* and is a Mahatma Gandhi Fellow of the American Academy of Political and Social Science.

The Acacia Strategy examines how race and equity intersect in the American higher education landscape. It is my hope that this publication will serve as a spring board for future educational dialogue and innovations.

Carolyn B. Rudd, Ed.D

President/CEO

CRP, Incorporated

Washington, DC

INTRODUCTION

The Acacia Strategy contains five essays on topics that are germane to American higher education today and what we believe are the connections for Historically Black Colleges and Universities (HBCUs) to begin a dialogue regarding innovative ideas and constructs within the HBCU community. It is our contention that historically black colleges can be a reservoir of untapped energy for innovative and collaborative models for solving some of the many problems that must be addressed by the higher education community and minority families. For well over a century, African American higher education institutions have produced world class leaders and creative minds that have changed society.

The essays are concerned with new models in teaching and learning; precisely how to deal with the education pipeline; the creation of a new kind of student ideal, how to make HBCUs the center of building sustainable communities; and ways to redefine race in the 21st century. All of these are critical issues that are now in play in American higher education. The work does not particularly look at secondary education, but two of the papers, one on teaching and learning and the other on education pipeline, are specifically geared to secondary education.

Why did we do these papers? It was the request of Dr. Joyce Payne of the Thurgood Marshall Scholarship Fund. Dr. Payne felt that the African American higher education community needed to be more focused in its dialogue and discernment regarding where and how HBCUs fit in the present education discourse. The underlying questions in the discussion of reform in education in America are the efficiency of the systems and its outcomes. In many ways, the African American population figures highly in both. The idea of the efficiencies of education takes us along two avenues. One, the need and the necessity to understand the duplication of services found in the State System of Higher Education among the State black and white higher education institutions. Many legislatures are voicing their opinions and working toward defining these black schools as an unnecessary financial burden to the state because of perceived duplication of two services.

And in the secondary world, there is the question of adeptness of secondary education personnel to deliver quality outcomes. Politicians, businessmen, and some educational leaders, have expressed their dissatisfaction regarding the dismal outcomes that many young children of color demonstrate in both their ability to sustain themselves in secondary education and to finish, and then to go forward into higher education. Both issues can be found in the five papers, with solutions. The amplification of a voice has not occurred in the past demonstrates both the practical application of knowledge that many HBCUs have done historically and could do today, and how these schools could be involved in closing the education gap in their own way. We believe that HBCUs today have extremely viable researched-based and evidence-based practices that could be put into play if there were major collaborations between the American higher education system and HBCUs.

Efficient use of resources lay with the issues involved in the financial stability of the nation's public and private institutions. We are continually reminded of the high cost of education, and the ineffective graduates they produce. The cost of education is presently overwhelming for all American families. There is the prospect that the working poor are completely priced out of the education market, and the middle class is in debt, well beyond their means to educate their children.

"College is outrageously expensive. Four years at an elite, private school such as the University of Chicago or Stanford costs more than a quarter of a million dollars. A degree from a more-affordable state school, like the College of William & Mary or the University of California, Berkeley, still costs around $100,000, even for in-state students, who pay less in tuition.

Is it worth it? For many students, the answer is probably not—unless they are accomplished enough to be accepted by one of the schools ranked near the top of Forbes' annual list of America's 650 Top Colleges.

The rankings, which are compiled exclusively for Forbes by the Washington, DC- based Center for College Affordability and Productivity, focus on the things that matter the most to students: quality of teaching, great career prospects, high graduation rates and low levels of debt. They do not attempt to assess a school's reputation, nor are they a measure of academic selectively, and we pointedly ignore any metrics that would encourage schools to engage in wasteful spending.

The rankings are based on five general categories: postgraduate success (32.5%), which evaluates alumni pay and prominence; student satisfaction (27.5%), which includes professor evaluations and freshman – to sophomore – year retention rates; debt (17.5%), which penalizes schools for high student debt loads and default rates; four-year graduation rates (11.25%); and competitive awards (11.25%), which rewards schools whose students win prestigious scholarships and fellowships like the Rhodes, Marshall and Fulbright or go on to earn PhD's".[1]

Based on those rankings, the number one college in America is Williams College, a small private college located in Massachusetts. The top black college is Fisk University, a small private college sited in Tennessee. Based on the five qualities stated above, only a handfull of HBCUs made the list. Most public schools fall behind the nation's private schools. Those elements capture the conceptual issues that are pushing reform in the United States today.

NOTE

[1]Noer, Michael (2012). America's Top Colleges.
Forbes, Retrieved August 8, 2012 from http://www.forbes.com/sites/michaelnoer/2012/08/01/americas-top-colleges-2/

FOUNDATION

MODELS OF EDUCATION

If nothing else, those ratings beg for clarification of the mission of the institutions and of American education in general. It does appear that America is moving down a road towards education only for the sake of business and job placement. If that is the mission of American higher education and American education in general, then it should be stated. Parents and students have the right to know where they are sending their children and what to expect from their educational experiences.

To date, one of the major emphasis of the Obama administration is to place a huge amount of money, $8 billion or more, into community colleges (See Appendix A). Community colleges have been and are a conduit for the development of needed skills and work-ready certificates and diplomas, all of which are necessary and must be applauded. However, at the same time, the black higher education system is suffering from a lack of finances and resources. It may be that they are seen as irrelevant to the present state of affairs, when in fact; these schools have produced the overwhelming majority of African American college graduates and created the African American middle class.

The point being, there has been a continuous discussion regarding whether one is educated for skills or for citizenship development and preparation to become a functional and effective member of society. These two important questions are back on the table again, but in a different guise. How do we address this? A reasoned response to the administration's desire to educate more Americans came from two educational leaders, Johnny C. Taylor of the Thurgood Marshall Scholarship Fund and Dr. Michael Lomax of the United Negro College Fund expressed,

> "Everybody who cares about getting young people the education they need, and that we as a nation need them to have, cheered yesterday's announcement by the Obama administration of the latest round of winners in the "Race to the Top" competitive education reform grant program.
>
> Thanks to Race to the Top funding, public school students in nine states and the District of Columbia will graduate from high school far better prepared for the college education they need to launch their careers. So important is college to our national economic strength that President Obama has committed the country to regaining world leadership in the proportion of citizens with college degrees.
>
> But despite the Obama administration's pledge to increase the number of American college graduates, it has not so far instituted or even proposed an initiative that brings to college education the much needed incentive to invigorate that Race to the Top has provided in pre-college education. The country especially needs innovative ways to help African-American, Hispanic American and other minority students get to and

through college. The United States is rapidly becoming a majority-minority country with a majority-minority workforce. Simply put, a large portion of our future teachers, doctors, scientific researchers and political leaders – in fact, a large portion of almost every fast-growing career category –will come from communities of color. But our national record of graduating minority students – especially minority students from low-income families – lags far behind the national need for minority college graduates. The national college graduation rate for all students is 55.9 percent. The African-American college graduation rate is 23 percent lower, at just 43 percent.

If only there were colleges that were up to the challenge posed by the nation's needs and president's ambitious goals-- colleges dedicated to the education of low-income African-Americans, colleges that know what it takes to get minority students into college and through college.

In fact, there are more than 100 colleges and universities with exactly that experience and exactly that tradition. They are America's historically black colleges and universities. And as the presidents of UNCF, the United Negro College Fund, which represents the nation's private HBCUs, and TMCF, the Thurgood Marshall College Fund, which represents our country's public HBCUs, we are volunteering our networks of colleges to serve as engines of innovation to meet this urgent national need.

UNCF and TMCF are prepared to pledge to the president and the country that America's HBCUs will produce for the economy 110,000 additional career-ready college graduates by 2020. And we are calling on the nation's corporations and foundations, and the federal government itself, to invest in these colleges and universities, as they have invested in preschool-through-high school education. We call on the country to invest in these young people, not just until they turn 18, but through college graduation. And we urge the country, starting with the federal government as lead investor, to invest in the economy by supporting the expansion in capacity that will be needed to help meet the president's goal."[1]

This is a straightforward, well thought out, and rational approach from two education leaders who understand that the proposition can be implemented.

One historic example of innovation of the highest order, and still works today is the Hampton-Tuskegee model. This model of education was created by two men, Samuel Chapman Armstrong and Booker T. Washington. Armstrong was the white director of Tuskegee Institute and its founding president, and Booker T. Washington was his most prominent student who worked under Armstrong. They created and expanded the model. The model combined both academic and manual training along with social training into a three-year curriculum. The curriculum included reading, language, math, history, and writing, but it also encompassed commercial, agricultural and mechanical courses, as well as the basics of living in the modern society.

This model of education was heavily funded by white philanthropists and industrialists, and many criticized it because it emphasized a type of education that these men thought people coming directly out of slavery needed. It was innovative and was the first time education had been done in that way. Few people gave Armstrong and Washington the credit they deserved. These strong institutions have grown, and many developed into major universities and also been the backbone of the black education experience for the last 170 years.

Currently, two modern models exist. The most promising is named Linking Historically Black Colleges and Universities with Community Colleges, created by Dr. Jacquelyn Madry-Taylor, advisor for Research and Program Development at the United Negro College Fund (UNCF) Special Programs Corporation, and The Links Incorporated. Recently funded by Lumina Foundation, this program is a collaboration between The Links and the National Association of Equal Opportunity and Higher Education, the UNCF Negro College Fund, and the UNCF Special Programs Corporation.

A model of collaboration will be developed and implemented that can be used to increase the number of community college students that are graduates from HBCUs. The specific goal is to increase the graduation rate of community college students, to increase the number of community college students that transfer to HBCUs, and to encourage greater collaboration between community colleges and HBCUs; thereby increasing the graduation rates of HBCUs. Five states are targeted, including Kentucky, Mississippi, North Carolina, Texas, and Virginia to pair community colleges with the HBCUs in their states.

This proposal is not only pioneering, it is far-seeing and provides the necessary relationship and the formulation that will be critical to not only produce the number of graduates that the President wants, but to establish the precedent of major black institutions collaborating with community colleges in their region. The same kind of visionary step must be made between major white universities and HBCUs.

This philosophy is developed in the essay "Education and Business Structuring the African American Student Pipeline" incorporated into this volume. It is a keystone in creating the kind of energy that will be necessary to put the education system into a balance for students of African descent, and can possibly lead to outcomes that education experts expect from a strong system of education.

The second extremely innovative model in Europe is a model of education that could certainly assist in the reformation and revamping of HBCUs for today's demands of efficiency and strong world class outcomes. This model can be found in Denmark at Aalborg University (See Appendix B).

"Aalborg University (AAU) is intentionally renowned as a leading educational institution within Problem Based Learning (PBL). Through problem based learning AAU wished to secure flexible interaction between theory and practice in the programmes. One of the principles of the PBL model is the fact that the students work on a problem oriented basis and complete projects of an advanced academic standard.

The research based programs at Aalborg University provide the students with a competence profile which is in high demand in the business world. Within all main areas, AAU offers academic programmes, including elite programmes and profession programmes, adapted to the needs of students as well as of the private and public sectors."[2]

Problem based learning is internationally recognized as a cutting edge learning experience. It seems particularly well suited for American HBCUs or possibly a consortium of these schools with American businesses and educational institutions (See Appendix B).

Sometimes remarkable programs come and go. We lose them, and yet they could have been of upmost importance to all that we do. One such program was the University of the District of Columbia – Lorton Prison Program. Operated by the University via an inter-agency funding program between the District of Columbia (D.C.) government and the University, the program was composed of both vocational and academic preparation.

"The college program was established in 1968 with Federal City College and Washington Tech. When the program first started student-inmates were bused to the campuses each day. They participated in Student Government and all campus activities including sports. Once the inmates broke the trust this was stopped but the program continued. The professor went to the prison and they were no longer active in campus activities. They could earn a variety of Associate Degrees but were limited to urban studies for the Bachelor's degree. The vocational program (non-credit) began in the 1990s. The vocational program staff was waived, certified or journeymen and the programs were

apprenticeship programs. The program was under Continuing
Education so we offered Dental Lab (prosthesis, teeth, dentures,
etc.), Electrical, Plumbing, Auto Mechanics, Computer Science,
Basic Business (keyboarding, filing, etc.) Bricklaying, Carpentry,
Graphic Arts."[3]

Assisted by the inmate students in 1983, Dr. Gilda Moss
Haber conducted an evaluation of the program. The study
was entitled "An Evolution of the University of the District
of Columbia and D.C. Department of Corrections: Lorton
Prison College Program at Lorton Correctional Facility."
Dr. Haber worked with two groups of male residents.

"This is a study comparing two (2) groups of male residents
in a correctional institution under the D.C. Department of
Corrections at Lorton, Virginia. The two (2) groups of residents
being compared are those with and those without a UDC college
education. We shall call the group without a college education,
the non-UDC group and those with UDC college education we
shall refer to as the UDC group, or sample. By UDC education,
we refer to the education provided to those eligible, at Lorton,
through and by the University of the District of Columbia. UDC
has been offering a degree program at Lorton since 1969.

Dr. Haber concluded that the non-UDC respondents appear to
be men who have begun a criminal career early on in life,
beginning with lesser offenses, perhaps, by continuing to commit
offenses and returning repeatedly to a correctional center. They
have also grown up with a number of male relatives who have
also been incarcerated throughout their lives. We suggested that
the non-UDC men appear to come from, and continue to
participate in, a "criminal culture" and to be career criminals.
The fact that they have stronger sociometric ties with the street
than the UDC men tends to support this picture.

Conversely, the UDC man commits his first offense at a later
age than the non-UDC man. It is more often an isolated, if
serious offense, with mitigating factors so that he has one
sentence, for a serious crime, but due to mitigating factors, a
shorter sentence. During his stay at Lorton he receives

comparatively few visits from friends, or even relatives, from the street; often expresses the wish to cut himself off from such ties, and forms ties, instead with others of his dormitory and in particular, we believe, with members of his dormitory who are also members of the UDC program and who are often in his classes.

Add to this, the earlier picture we described, whereby more often, the UDC man comes from a more educated father and mother, and if married, has a more educated wife; his parents, wife and he, himself, have worked more often in white-collar jobs; and he has higher aspirations and hopes of continued freedom upon release than has the non-UDC man.

We tested and found support for seven (7) hypotheses:

1. That the UDC sample perseveres more than the non-UDC sample in achieving goals, particularly in education.
2. That the UDC resident comes from a less culturally deprived family.
3. That the UDC resident values his education and its positive impact on his future more than the non-UDC resident.
4. The UDC resident has a better work history than the non-UDC resident, which in itself is a measure of more probable future success in the work field.
5. The UDC resident, unlike the non-UDC resident, is not usually a career criminal; nor does he come from a family with other members of the family incarcerated, although he has often committed a serious crime, though with mitigating factors and, therefore, has a shorter sentence than men in the non-UDC group.
6. The reference and friendship group of the UDC residents is based on other upwardly mobile residents; whereas, the non-UDC group more often maintains ties to the street.
7. The UDC group scored higher than the non-UDC group on the POI, the maximization of potential.

Thus, we propose that there are two (2) types of residents at Lorton, completely different from one another, represented by the non-UDC men repeaters, career criminals with low chances of being rehabilitated, and the UDC prototype who has a high likelihood, yet to be tested, of leaving Lorton a better man than he came in and highly unlikely to be a recidivist after release.

If a UDC college education does have these salutary effects and also draws to it the most promising young men with a fairly good family background, considering the fact that they mostly come from an economically and culturally deprived area, then it is well worth the financial investment involved in giving them a college education. If we prove our hypothesis in the next phase of the research, comparing integration into the community and reduction in recidivism among the UDC group, then, this research will document the high evaluation of the college program in a correctional setting. All kinds of policy implications would be involved, such as an increase in higher education at correctional institutions, and the ability to pre-test residents as they come in, as to whether they have the characteristics we have described above, which will make them good students, and law abiding citizens upon release"[4] (See Appendix C and D).

The policy implications are obvious. The program was closed by the DC Government in the late 1990s.

MISSIONS

Reform seems now to drive all of the various decisions that we are witnessing in education. One of the most overlooked ideals is something that can only be described as a life or death omission, and that is the well-defined mission of education in America today. The mission will determine the outcome.

Without a concrete idea of following and understanding the mission of education, we will fall prey to what happened in Washington, D.C. In the early 1970s, Congress passed legislation, DC Law 1-36, that called for a system to consolidate all post-secondary education in the District of Columbia. In that consolidation, it required public higher education institutions to merge to conserve financing, bolster academic offerings and become more effective. Over a period of several years, a single system was established from three separate institutions, converging into the University of the District of Columbia. It was a hard-fought battle, and remained one of the major dramas within the District of Columbia, in both political and social life for the last 30 years (See Appendix E).

Just when the consolidation was complete and there was an understanding within the University of what ought to occur, forces came on the scene, generally driven by business and politics, to decouple the school. A community college was created, even though it already existed within the consolidated University.

From that approach, young people could go from their Associate in Arts and Associate in Science degrees directly into the university, requiring no articulation plan because it was built into the department in which they were a part. For instance, nursing students could go directly into the Bachelor of Science degree program without transferring to a separate entity.

After 30 years of hard work, the entire process had been pulled apart to create a community college; it was the new thing. Politicians and businessmen thought they could acquire new workers, even though the reason was unclear as to why the same workers could not be found in the old UDC academic structure; costing less money in a time when there was fiscal austerity. Courses offered at the Community College were not all new. They were the same courses that the university departments offered and managed. There is little that is new at DC Community College that was not at UDC. And so, there were certainly those who voiced their opinion that the destruction or pulling apart of that one section of the school would then destroy the upper college or the University of the District of Columbia (See Appendix F).

There will be a push to remove the law school from the university as well, once again creating three separate institutions with three separate budgets, even though they may be consolidated within one general budget. Presidents or chancellors of each of those new higher education institutions will be necessary.

"Somewhere along the way this simply illustrates the loss of the legislative, social and educational mission of the University. Consequently anything can occur, including changing the founding date of the consolidated university from its actual consolidation in 1976, to the founding date of one of the three predecessor institutions which was founded in1851, all in an attempt to destroy its present identity and misrepresent its urban mission which is a legislative mandate. DC law 1-36"

The point is to address the idea that each time a new person appears on the scene with another magic bullet, everything will change. A community college might be established instead of an evaluation as to how effective consolidation had been through looking at the graduates of the school and learning what they accomplished. There might have been a completely different outcome had this been initially done.

This is important for not only Washington, D.C., but it is crucial as a reminder for all of higher education not to destroy black colleges at a moment when they may be one of the most valuable innovative engines for higher education. Ill-advisedly, once businessmen and politicians get ahead of steam, it is difficult to reverse their actions.

We need a reasoned and rational conversation about the mission of American education. It can be and probably should be a hybrid between creating what Émile Durkheim would call moral education, what Jean Jacques Rousseau would call the social contract or citizenship education, and what John Dewey would call pragmatism. The idea being there must be some braiding of various philosophical ideas in these complex times to create a system of education that deals with the moral issues and questions of the day that deal with grassroots democracy and citizenship as a serious business for all Americans, and to learn about the relationships that we must have toward one another in this democracy. It must be pragmatic enough to develop the necessary intellectual arena for both philosophical ideas and practical skills for career readiness.

I believe one of the most interesting factors in black higher education has been the understanding that both Booker T. Washington and the Hampton-Tuskegee model and W. E. B. Du Bois, who was a product of the Fisk model of classical education, have melded into present-day institutions that not only produce intellectually alive and gifted young students, but also young men and women who are in the workforce doing both practical and skilled technological work as well as philosophical and scientific endeavors. Overtime, they have come together to be the black higher education system in America today. And this is one of the most pragmatic features that HBCUs can bring to the world of higher education; how these two bitterly-opposed education philosophies have become comfortable with each other and are intertwined in the development and education of African American students.

W. E. B. Du Bois wrote of a particular refinement about education and of individuals after slavery,

"This the missionaries of '68 soon saw, and if effective industrial and trade schools were impracticable before the establishment of a common school system, just as certainly no adequate common schools could be founded until there were teachers to teach them. Southern whites would not teach them; Northern whites in sufficient numbers could not be had. If the Negro was to learn, he must teach himself, and the most effective help that could be given him was the establishment of schools to train Negro teachers. This conclusion was slowly but surely reached by every student of the situation until simultaneously, in widely separated regions, without consultation or systematic plan, there arose a series of institutions designed to furnish teachers for the untaught. Above the sneers of critics at the obvious defects of this procedure must ever stand in one crushing rejoinder: in a single generation they put thirty thousand black teachers in the South; they wiped out the illiteracy of the majority of the black people in the land, and they made Tuskegee possible.
    Such higher training schools tended naturally to deepen broader development: at first they were common and grammar schools, then some became high schools. And finally, by 1900, some thirty-four had one year or more of studies of college grade. This development was reached with different degrees of speed in different institutions: In all cases the aim was identical. To maintain the standards of the lower training by giving teachers and leaders the best practicable training; and above all to furnish the black world with adequate standards of human culture and lofty ideals of life." [5]

The point of this certainly shows the animosity that the two systems had toward one another, but it also demonstrated that the redesign of education to fit the needs and secure the future of African Americans was the essential factor for both. Their job was to simply work to build the infrastructure upon which these new citizens could participate.

Those leaders understood that there was a need to redefine the mission of education and how that education would affect the African American. They could not approach it in the same way as Europeans. They needed a total uplift from the bottom to make the illiterate literate, and in many cases, that exact issue faces the African American community today... how to make the illiterate literate once again.

THE REDEFINING SOLUTION

Certainly, it will be key for a dialogue to be constructed between the American higher education system and the HBCU education system. There are four specific redefining solutions that must be created to help in this dialogue: a think-tank, clearinghouse, grassroots leadership academy, and delivery system. Undoubtedly, the complexity of all of these issues must go up against an already established system for creating policy and aligning policy issues with political outcomes. Nothing in America is simple, and so it requires a strong voice, one that will not go unheard, but be amplified and taken seriously.

There is a need to establish a comprehensive think-tank of scholars and practitioners that will collect, study and disseminate information online. The think-tank would compile best practice and lessons learned to bring about new and serviceable knowledge to school systems, higher education institutions, and other education arenas. A think-tank could answer how to train the poor for work in a global economy, what skills are needed and how to provide them, and how the poor, underclass, and working poor can compete in the global context.

A think-tank would contain a national clearing house to collect studies, reports, polls, and other relevant data. This material can be used for research and replication, nationally and locally. It would develop benchmark data report and historical archival materials to be used in program development and proposal development for local and national groups and organizations.

The generation of extraordinary men and women that developed many of the working and innovative programs in black higher education are beginning to retire. The training of a new generation of civic community social entrepreneurs is a must. "Grassroots civic leadership is the empowerment of individuals: parents, teachers, ministers, and young people, to take control of their lives and communities."[6] A grassroots leadership academy would establish a curriculum and an online course of study, as well as providing mentors for those wanting to become community leaders that work with fragile families as educational coordinators. The leadership academy would coordinate five issues as the framework for a multi-generational change process: a national literacy development initiative; a national healthy lifestyles communication public program; a national anti-drug campaign; an economic literacy campaign and; ethical and spiritual dialogues.

EDUCATION SOCIAL INFRASTRUCTURE

Education social infrastructure would support coordination of a safety net for at risk youth, particularly those from families of poverty, and addiction. It would be the portal for resource data to increase youth's access to information concerning educational opportunities, substance abuse prevention, bullying, physical and mental health and social services. The network would also be the place where parents, education specialists, health professionals, social workers, pastors, schools, or mentors could access resource information to help youth during emergencies and crises that require immediate interventions. Additionally, the network would include information that professionals can use to address behavioral, physical or sociological problems that are potential barriers to the educational and social development of our youth. The purpose of the network is to increase:

- online access to educational opportunities;
- substance abuse prevention and treatment policies across multiple sectors;
- cross-sector coordination and safety-net opportunities for youth who are victims of bullying;
- social inclusion of at risk youth; and
- substance abuse prevention and treatment information to at risk youth and their families.

If education is to be redefined, the mission of education must be practical and make sense to the majority of Americans so that they can participate in making it work, and prepare their students to complete. It also must define a dynamic public ideal, an all-encompassing uplift that Du Bois talked about that occurred after slavery; allowing a generation of illiterates to train themselves and brought a stupendous uplift to the overwhelming majority of African Americans at that time.

It may seem somewhat pedantic to outline so many things that will be necessary to bring about a new mission, but the problem today is that without creating a multi-faceted and multi-pronged approach to the mission, we will once again slip into skills or citizenship; that need not happen. They can be combined, and there are ways of preparing young people to raise the level of their education and outcomes for the nation.

NOTES

[1]Taylor, Johnny C. & Lomax, Dr. Michael (2010). American Needs More College Grads: How HBCUs Can Help. The Grio, NBC News Retrieved from http://thegrio.com/2010/08/25/america-needs-more-college-grads-how-hbcus-can-help/

[2]Aulborg University Denmark, Education and Programmes offered at AAU (2012). Retrieved from www.en.aau.dk/education+%26+programs/

[3]Carter, Saundra Majid (2012) Memorandum. April 10,
   2012, (p.1)

[4]Haber, Gilda Moss, Ph.D. (1983, March). An Evaluation of
   the University of the District of Columbia and DC
   Department of Corrections Lorton Prison Colleges
   program at Lorton Correctional Facility. Paper presented
   at the national meeting of the Academy of Criminal
   Justice Sciences, San Antonio, Texas. March 18, 1983.
   (pp. 40-42)

[5]Du Bois, W.E.B (1902). Of the Training of Black Men,
   The Atlantic Online, originally published in The
   Atlantic Monthly Volume XC - September 1902 –
   DXXXIX.   Retrieved   from
   http://www.theatlantic.com/past/docs/unbound/flashbks/
   blacked/dutrain.htm

[6]Austin, Bobby William (1996). Repairing the breach:
   Report of the national task force on African American
   men and boys. Dillon, Colorado: Alpine Guild, Inc (p.
   80)

THE ACACIA STRATEGY

The Acacia Strategy is a series of discussion papers around issues of innovation and sustainability for America's HBCUs. The focus of the strategy is to develop a series of overarching themes around which CRP, Inc. (CRP) and these institutions can create an ongoing conversation on the innovative academic work of these colleges, and to find ways to sustain this work. The Acacia Strategy is centered on the fact that retention, access and accountability rest on the need for a policy shift that is cultural in nature. The papers in the strategy emphasize this and recommend techniques that create the desired outcomes to give our students the best opportunities for educational success.

There are four sub-strategies that comprise the Acacia Strategy. First, the nation's HBCUs have a track record and a wealth of information. They must share with each other and the larger education community and assume the role by documenting and reporting historical and present day successes. Second, a new approach to teaching and learning is needed and those models are available and being used in our colleges. In addition, one of the most pressing needs for HBCUs is to form partnerships and regional collaborations to build and sustain governmental and business support. If we are to be successful, it is essential that HBCUs have technological infrastructure investment by government and industry as it relates to education pipeline issues. Last, we must realign our thinking on poverty and race as determinants of success. We do this by creating new narratives that are viewed from a perspective other than a deficit model.

On the Serengeti, in Eastern Africa, there grows a magnificent tree named the Acacia. It is also called the umbrella tree for its shape. It branches form what appears to be an open umbrella over the Serengeti savannah, and is important for the savannah's stability. It is able to withstand heat and cold, with temperatures of 120 degrees Fahrenheit to below freezing at night. It also survives without a constant water source, within rocky soil, and it provides a great measure of substance and protection as well as a sure resting place for animals and humans alike. The Acacia of America is sometimes called the locust tree, and can be found in almost every part of the globe. They are adaptable, and grow in soil somewhat different from their origination. In many ways, America's HBCUs have this adaptability, dependability and sustainability.

The history of America's public and private black colleges reflects the segregated system that was in place from the inception of the nation until the 1960s. There are 105 HBCUs today. They are composed of two main categories, private colleges and universities and public institutions. The bulk of the private schools were founded first following the Civil War, including Lawler Cheyney University of Pennsylvania, established in 1837, Lincoln University established in 1854 and Wilberforce, established in 1854. The majority of these schools were founded by religious denominations, among them, the Congregational church, the African Methodist Episcopal Church, the African Methodist Episcopal Zion and the Baptist denomination.

The first group of land grant colleges under the Morrill Act of 1862 provided both land and money for the development of the land grant system of colleges. In the North and the West, African Americans participated in the public educational process. The 17 southern states excluded blacks from their land grant colleges.

Thus, a second Morrill Act of 1890 was passed, establishing the separate land grant college system for blacks who had been omitted from the earlier land grant act. The Act continues to this day, and has been the major educational conduit for African Americans. According to the U.S. Department of Education in a report on HBCUs, these HBCUs, both private and public, accounted for 13 percent of black higher education enrollment. The issue papers that comprise **The Acacia Strategy** serve several purposes:

a. Provide venues for discussion around various issues that are currently in play with respect to higher education in the United States;

b. Cover specific topics that have relevance to HBCUs;

c. Speak specifically, generally and boldly to the ideas, possibilities, vision and mission of public higher education history and policy;

d. Explore daring inventive areas based on the tremendous work already accomplished by HBCUs;

e. Provide a sound basis for establishing a federal agenda in the coming decades;

f. Create a contextual framework for discussing issues by the fund, and establishing a coordinated collaborative dialogue between the nation's black colleges and the general American higher education community;

g. Facilitate our funding strategies from both public and private sources over the next decade;

h. Establish the voice of HBCUs in the public media arena by providing perspective and analysis from our distinct point of view.

PUBLIC DISCOURSE

To begin this challenging process, CRP has implemented an Online Think Tank. This operation will launch our public discourse in the field of educational policy as a thought leader and as one voice for HBCUs. This concept would lead directly to the establishment of an innovative vehicle for educational development for African Americans, and as a clearinghouse for innovative educational thought.

It is time to begin a process of reflection and thinking and development of the possibilities of how to understand the moment of truth that we now face and how the black colleges of America can provide both answers and a place where discussions can take place that will provide answers for the nation. America's HBCUs are the place of thinkers, scholars and leaders who, most of all are people of compassion and empathy. As a group, African Americans have created a world class culture that has grown in the U.S. and made for itself a model of what the Acacia tree is to the Serengeti.

The papers that are in this discussion should help us to begin to clarify and frame exactly how the black colleges of America become a central platform for the dialogue of *men and women thinking* today, as heirs to Dr. King's world house. They can be counted on to design a broad vision for America's educational enterprise. In an article by Dr. Ivy Nelson, "The Future Teaching Research and Public Service Mission of Historically Black Public University," we note the following:

"Today, the world's 165 independent nations are tightly interlocked. What happens in the furthest corner of the world now touches everyone instantly. Through technology we share a common classroom and the world has become a threatening and unsafe place. If historically black public universities are not utilized and involved in providing experiences that make students see beyond themselves and better understand the interdependent nature of our world, then America has squandered one of its greatest resources;"

"...Thus the need and place for historically black public colleges is quite apparent if one considers the projected increase in minority enrollment as the only factor. But if one considers the total needs of higher education, then higher education must also provide: 1) Places to accommodate by the year 2010 approximately the same number of students as were enrolled in 1978, it will not make sense to substantially reduce the capacity only to have to recreate it again in the near future; 2) Institutions representing at least the degree of diversity we have today. The United States is an intricate mosaic of races, ethnic groups, religions, occupational pursuits, styles of life and is becoming even more so, at least in occupational pursuits and styles of life, Institutions, like historically black public land grant universities, that pay attention to these diversities will be at least equally needed in the future as in the past; 3) Capabilities for greater equality of opportunity; and 4) Capacities for providing service to the surrounding community."[1]

Dr. Nelson's statement provides the rationale for the entire educational structure to regard the needs and opportunities that the public black college offers America. She also places before the public black college establishment the task of what should be the vision for the next several decades. The public black college network must foster openness, dialogue, transparency, collaboration, and critical thought around the global nature of our lives, as well as the responsibilities of our institutions to prepare our administration, faculties, staff and students to participate and lead in this present arena.

NOTE

[1]Koepplin, Leslie W. & Wilson, David A. (1985) The Future of State Universities: Issues in Teaching, Research and Public Service, Ed. Rutgers University, 1985. (pp. 130-131).

EDUCATION POLICY DIRECTIONS

There are six policy directions that HBCUs should pursue as a result of the development of the Acacia Strategy.

TEACHING AND LEARNING

HBCUs must focus on the innovative approaches to teaching and learning that are being developed, with an eye toward replication of proven models such as the Gateway Academic Program (GAP) at the University of the District of Columbia. Specifically, the GAP is a summer program developed by an interdisciplinary team led by Dr. Daryao Khatari, a physicist; Dr. Anne Hughes, a sociologist; and Dr. Brenda Brown, a mathematician. The program produced astounding results. In one summer it brought low achieving students in math and English into the general academic curriculum. That is tangible proof that the achievement gap can be closed. The program rests on the comprehensive training program to teach professors how to administer the physics-based program as a cross disciplinary academic exercise. The new pedagogy is central to all of the nations' pipeline issues. The GAP program represents a reform of the curriculum and new innovation in teaching and learning.

REFOCUSING POVERTY AND RACE

Poverty is one of the main reasons for the inability of youngsters to finish their education, and causes those who are in the education system to lag behind. Poverty plays a central role in whether or not a family can afford higher education. HBCUs will pursue collaborative partnerships with national governmental and corporate entities in the establishment of a Commission to ferret out the best and most effective avenues to alleviate poverty as a deterrent to educational achievement.

In like manner, HBCUs will lead an internal dialogue within the public black college network to understand scientific developments and anthropological discoveries that are redefining the idea of race through DNA research. This dialogue is a teachable moment. It will expose students to the academic disciplines that are making these discoveries, understanding the various branches of science, the world of anthropology and the study of mathematics and linguistics. This policy will set the stage for student self-discovery, new vocational horizons and a sense of global human kinship.

REGIONALISM

HBCUs should develop a set of regional academic collaborates. These collaborative entities will be forums for discussion and development of partnerships to strengthen families and the institutions that serve them. The regional concept will engage the public, private, religious, education and community-based organizational sectors. They will provide the stage for the creation of sustainable plans to prepare families to access higher education and to finance the choice.

The development of Family Focused Education is significant to the regional concept. This concept will be developed within the proposed Du Bois Marshall University College, an online general studies set of seminars and instructional questions addressing the means to enter, finance and complete educational opportunities. Most importantly, it will also focus on how to discuss with the children in the family the same set of questions. Using the family as a teaching unit will enhance the effectiveness of the program; allowing the parents the opportunity to build the desire for education within the family. Educational counselors and professionals will be made available to make this comprehensive, yet simple to accomplish. The model will include a workbook/text and a DVD.

Financial literacy skill building will accompany the education guide. Including in the document are the basic scenarios for funding higher education. These programs will be geared toward helping families make financial decisions regarding educational opportunities.

The regional sustainability focus will necessitate the need for environmental impact studies on the health and welfare of families in the nation's major cities and in our rural communities where our institutions are located. In 1970 and in 1972, Congressional Hearings were held before the Select Committee on Nutrition and Human Needs and the Committee on Commerce, both in the U.S. Senate. These hearings were specific in their focus on the nation's poor and the urban environment. Much has happened, positive and negative, in the intervening 35 years since those hearings. The nation's HBCUs are calling for a new round of congressional hearings on the continuing impact of and concern for sustainable living conditions in our nation; with particular regard to communities of color in the U.S. and its effect on educational outcomes.

GLOBAL CITIZENS

The outcome of an education within the HBCU network of colleges will be to prepare students as global citizens. To this end, an alliance with private funders, government agencies and corporate sponsors will be necessary. The program will prepare students as well as graduates to engage the national, international and the local community as *bridge builders*. These students will be prepared in character and principled leadership studies, critical thinking, foreign language development, and international political and social studies. While it is envisioned that all students will be introduced to this model as determined by the individual colleges, CRP will work with the Presidents to make this a comprehensive and open opportunity.

TECHNOLOGICAL INFRASTRUCTURE

The development of a technological infrastructure linking the 47 institutions of black public higher education is a must for their continued growth and development, and to provide them with the ability to compete as a major educational platform for research, innovation and collaboration. This technological structure would be based in a proposed Du Bois Marshall University College. This comprehensive technological structure would connect faculties and staff, general curriculum offerings, continuing education, research and development, and public policy initiatives. It would support, in multiple ways, long term research endeavors and spur collaborative activities with universities around the nation. Within the sustainability for families' arena, it would support readily available continuing interventions with solution based models for replication, lessons learned, best practices, personal mentors and a clearinghouse of grassroots/community-based organizations engaged in education and community development.

In a series of technology driven data banks, replication sites and personal life plan development systems, the Education/Social Infrastructure will act as an education network for learning and research. Using cloud computing techniques, this education infrastructure would be an organizing principle around which major collaborative efforts could be facilitated by the HBCUs, government, industry and the philanthropic world.

THE MISSION OF EDUCATION

Critical to the work and outcomes that we hope for within the Public Black College Network, is the necessity to define the overall mission of American Higher Education and specifically, the mission and role that Public Black Colleges and Private Black Colleges will play within the national milieu in the 21st Century. What is the purpose for education? It is the question that all Americans must ask and answer. We are no exception. We will identify ourselves in relationship to the defined national mission as we help to craft it in accordance with our own historic status, present needs and future vision.

GROUNDED REALITY

All of these policy directives are grounded in our research and development. But, they are also geared to the Education agenda as established by President Obama. The policy directives emphasize access and educational financial issues as well as the need for reform and innovation.

TEACHING AND LEARNING IN THE 21ST CENTURY:

WILL THE NATION'S PUBLIC BLACK COLLEGES DEFINE THE TEACHING MODEL OF THE FUTURE?

The future of the national desire to reform and improve the American education system rests on the shoulders of the American teaching force. Consequently, we must discover a new way to prepare teachers and a reform methodology for the pedagogy of teaching and learning. In this paper we try and answer these questions, by featuring a program called the GAP program created by three University of the District of Columbia professors.

The concepts of teaching and learning today are very much at the heart of the entire agenda regarding the reform of education in the United States. Billions of dollars have been already spent or allocated in the push to make America's schools *world class*. Needless to say, it would be foolhardy to really believe that the public schools of

America are such total failures. They could not possibly be. It is more that the public schools have received such a bad public relations hit along with a devastating political black-eye that it's hard to do battle with those who seem to think that nothing good comes out of the school system if it cannot be tested and measured. We should acknowledge, however, that there are a tremendous number of underperforming schools in the nation.

Probably, if all the reform measures or standards had been in place 100 or even 50 years ago, where would we be? Would we know for sure that schools in other countries really are superior to ours? What their students represent is the ability to very definitely take and do well on a test. Whether or not it demonstrates their actual knowledge or proficiency in the subject matter is another question.

Scholars are now beginning to raise issues regarding testing and measurement. We do not need to dismantle the public education system which has been the great equalizer in American society or at least to push it totally into a test and measurement teaching pedagogy. One of the early education reformers was Diane Ravitch. Ms. Ravitch's new book entitled, "The Death and Life of the Great American School System," has this to say about the ideas that are

central to the school reform movement that is in full swing
in the United States today.

"...Education is the key to developing human capital. The
nature of our education system – whether mediocre or excellent –
will influence society far into the future. It will affect not only
our economy but also our civic and cultural life. A democratic
society cannot long sustain itself if its citizens are uninformed
and indifferent about its history, its government and the workings
of its economy. Nor can it prosper if it neglects to educate its
children in the principles of science, technology, geography,
literature and the arts. The great challenge to our generation is to
create a renaissance in education, one that goes well beyond the
basic skills that have recently been the singular focus of federal
activity, a renaissance that seeks to teach the best that has been
thought and known and done in every field of endeavor.

The policies we are following today are unlikely to improve
our schools. Indeed, much of what policymakers now demand
will very likely make schools less effective and many further
degrade the intellectual capacity of our citizenry. The schools
will surely be failures if students graduate knowing how to
choose the right option from four bubbles on a multi-choice test,
but unprepared to live fulfilling lives, to be responsible citizens,
and to make good choices for themselves, their families and our
society..."[1]

Ravitch continues,

"The fundamentals of good education are to be found in the
classroom, the home, the community and the culture, but
reformers in our time continue to look for shortcuts and quick
answers. Untethered to any genuine philosophy of education, our
current reforms will disappoint us, as others have in the past. We
will, in time, see them as distractions, wrong turns and lost
opportunities. It is time to reconsider not only the specifics of
current reforms but also our very definition of reform."[2]

In the face of such a dramatic series of statements, Diane
Ravitch is John the Baptist crying in the wilderness. For

someone to hear that we may be on the wrong track based on evidence and research studies that have looked at the various curriculum, teaching methods, pedagogy and a review of the schools that have been funded and started during this period of reform is devastating. This is not to say that all reform has been bad or is bad even though Ms. Ravitch seems to think that it has been devastatingly disappointing.

The upshot is how can the HBCU network bring to the fore a series of prospects that might be advantageous to, if not fulfilling the reform goal. The reform mission might be redirected so that the thrust of the movement is not so tied to math and science solely but to the development of the whole individual, and in our own way, the global individual who is prepared to take a leadership position in the world house as defined by Dr. King.

We see this as our mission. The quest for education by African-Americans has been informed by the various visions and visionaries who have brought African-Americans in just a few generations from slavery to the White House. This particular moment in time requires a thoughtful assessment of what the next level in education reform should look like and what shape it should take.

EDUCATION MISSION

Structurally, it seems that the quest for quality teachers and a sound pedagogy to prepare America's students is at the heart of the reform movement. Certainly, the mission for all of education in the United States requires some thought. At this moment there are a few people who would say that they have the answer. Therefore, it seems that this is one area where the nation and the many stakeholders who are so passionately invested in what happens to public education define for themselves a venue where they can talk and craft a genuine educational mission for the United States: a mission that is multifaceted and with many layers leading to one objective – the universal education of all American young people and the building of an educational structure that leverages every possible institution that has interest as a supporter and stakeholder in making this a reality.

Within the near future, it seems absolutely mandatory that a conference or at least a series of workshops on education mission in the United States be convened. This is a mandatory effort on the part of the black higher education establishment. Every series of statistical data published in the United States points to one glaring gap and that is the lagging educational scores of African-American children and adults. It should not be considered a national disgrace but a gigantic series of missed opportunities from the federal, state and local governments, that certain groups are having such a dismal educational experience.

This conference could be one of the first steps in planning how we attack this major issue. There are two arenas around which this mission would be crafted. At the center, would be teacher enhancement and development and pedagogical reform leading to a new teaching process and productivity for both learners and teachers.

Scholars agree that the literacy gap for children and youth is rooted in poverty. According to the National Center for Children in Poverty at the Mailman School of Public Health at Columbia University, nearly one in every five American children lives in poverty. Sixty-one percent of black children live in low income families, representing 6.4 million children, almost two-thirds of the population.

It is pretty clear where the problems start and why it exists – poverty. Poverty, which seems to be a dirty word these days, is the single best predictor of the lack of achievement and yet poverty is not a top priority on anyone's agenda today.

To be poor in 2010 is one's own fault. These ideas come out of the political conservative agenda of the '80s and '90s. People are poor because either they wish to be or they are too uninformed and unmotivated to do better. This is a very sad position for the world's lone super power to be in. It says much about who we are as a nation and it speaks volumes as to why we cannot close the education gap or do not have the will to close the gap. But we are aware of what must be done if we are to close the gap. There are workable solutions to alleviate the staggering poverty statistics in the United States – the university professionals within the HBCUs could provide the necessary scholarship and leadership to implement multiple solutions, based on lessons learned in our land grant efforts and best practice initiatives that are working across the nation.

IMPACT OF POVERTY

To add to this gloomy picture, look at an article on www.bloomberg.com dated September 10, 2009; reads:

"U.S. Poverty Rate Rises to 11-year High as Recession Takes a Toll. Poverty has risen from 12.5 percent to 13.2 percent for the nation as a whole, up from 35.9 million or 12.5 percent in 2003. There are 7.9 million families in poverty in 2004, up from 7.6 million in 2003. In 2004, the poverty rate declined for Asians, 9.8 percent in 2004, down from 11.8 percent in 2002;

remained unchanged for Hispanics, 21.9 percent and blacks 24.7 percent, and rose for non-Hispanic whites, 8.6 percent in 2004, up from 8.2 percent in 2003.

For all children under 18, both the 2004 poverty rate of 17.8 percent and the number in poverty, 13 million, were unchanged in 2003. The Midwest is the only region to show an increase in poverty, 11.6 percent in 2004 up from 10.7 percent in 2003. In 2004, the poverty rates for the Northwest 11.6 percent, the South 14.1 percent, and the West 12.6 percent were unchanged in 2003. The South continued to have the highest poverty rate in the nation."

Clearly, a picture emerges that poverty continues to grow in America. The number of children in poverty has certainly grown and it makes very little sense to talk about closing the education gap when the research finds poverty a key indicator for success or failure in the present education system. But could there be a workable, alternative option. We believe that two such options do exist. One, an extended definition of literacy and a redesign of a learning and teaching pedagogy that removes poverty as a stumbling block for success among poor students.

LITERACY

It is important to at least give some credence to new definitions of literacy. The general definition, of course, has been the ability to read and write and understand the written word in society and the level with which one does that with proficiency. There are also new definitions of literacy that can be used to create a larger arena for assessment of literacy skills.

A report prepared by the Village Foundation in 2000, listed nine definitions of literacy: emotional literacy, family literacy, information literacy, legal literacy, math literacy, media literacy, theoretical literacy, social literacy, and workplace literacy. This may seem elongated but it does offer a wide array of expectations for people who are struggling to attain literacy in society. All of these, of course, require the basic literacy skill – reading.

What these new expansions of literacy offer is the need to be proficient in how to read to understand one's medical records and directions for taking medication, reading and understanding one's legal issues, reading and understanding math related areas which influence comprehension of financial aspects of everyday living. Media literacy is certainly a necessary aspect to just about everything we do in America in both public and private life. The restructuring of America's educational system should in fact – particularly at the college level – take into effect these expanded literacy skills.

One-half of the mission equation is multiple "literacy's"; the other half is multiple intelligences. Howard Gardner's

Intelligence Reframed and the *Multiple Intelligences* offer an expanded view of intelligence that correlates very well with the expanded view of literacy. Multiple intelligences and multiple literacy definitions are keys to an enhanced and workable structure to re-envision and reformat the American educational structure and the delivery of that learning to multiple groups of students. An additional option is the Gateway Academic Program.

Can we reformat the delivery of teaching and learning today? The answer is that it already has been accomplished. It has been accomplished mainly through a program that might not recognize the terms of either expanded literacy or multiple intelligences but simply a new pedagogy and dedicated and mature learning styles of three professors at the University of the District of Columbia, and their program: the Gateway Academic Program. The three professors are Dr. Daryao S. Khatri, professor of physics; Dr. Anne O. Hughes, professor of sociology, retired; and Professor Brenda Brown. Professor Khatri is a physicist, Professor Hughes is a social scientist, and Professor Brown is a mathematician.

What they have done at the University of the District of Columbia is truly astounding. They have – probably against all odds – demonstrated that poverty itself may not be the defining factor or barrier to closing the gap in the critical educational skills that the school reform movement considers important – math and science. GAP does not discount poverty but the project works with individuals who are at least motivated and are already struggling in the system. They are not educational drop-outs where poverty may be the overriding factor.

Over the past two decades, through extensive research and work, GAP has successfully demonstrated that the high school disparities in math, reading and English, which most minority students are unable to master above the remedial level, can be closed during an intensive eight-week summer program. This seems almost impossible. According to research done on the program, it successfully eliminated the need for college remedial courses for between 70 percent and 80 percent of participating high school and entering freshman who were a part of the GAP program.

According to their success stories, five students who decided to major in math and math-related fields are on track to graduate in the typical four- or five-year period with bachelor's degrees. One student who started at the bottom of the ACCUPLACER testing spent the following summer at the national Fermilab as a student intern. Another student had been offered a full scholarship for both undergraduate and graduate work in physics. A third student who did not care about books at all cannot be seen on campus without a book anymore. A fourth student who started as a total failure in high school is on his way to becoming a physician. The fifth student who is a double major in psychology and physics is expected to graduate in a typical four- or five-year frame.

So what can produce these astounding results? In the GAP program, the retention rates are between 95 percent and 100 percent in Introductory College Physics 1 and 2: the national rate is between 25 and 40. The GAP program, through management and teaching strategies, transformed teaching skills of high school teachers and college faculty. There are reports of classroom retention in Chemistry I moving from 50 percent to 97 percent and student's success tripling from 30 percent to 90 percent. GAP offers two types of service: 1) intensive academic programs to overcome student deficiencies in algebra, reading and English; and, 2) teacher-faculty training for high school teachers and college students. It's a daily after-school three-hour-per-day intensive academic program for students are in high school and doing poorly in math, English and reading, and who want to graduate from high school rather than drop out, and a summer eight-week four-hour-per-day intensive academic program for students who graduated from high school but who will be required to take remedial math, reading and/or English courses prior to taking college level courses. For teachers, it is a two-week, six-hour-per-day enhancement training in the GAP pedagogy, which is offered in Washington, D.C. or at convenient locations; and a follow-up two-week mentoring program is offered throughout the whole semester. These teachers receive a GAP training certificate.

These are the basic core ingredients of the GAP and what are the results? GAP results for both pre- and post-test of all of the students by the National College Board ACCUPLACER for the past four summers starting in 2006 to the present are highlighted on their Web site. In basic math and introductory algebra, in the summer 2006 pilot program, 50 percent of students tested out of either one or both of the remedial math courses based on the College Board ACCUPLACER test; of those, 15 percent of the students decided to major in physics.

The summer '07 research reports 50 percent of the students tested out of both the remedial math courses thereby saving themselves one year of remedial course work; 31 percent tested out of one remedial math course thus avoiding a semester of remedial course work; 31

percent of the students decided to major in math, physics and chemistry; 82 percent of these students are still enrolled in college.

In 2008, 68 percent of the students tested out of both remedial math courses; 16 percent tested out of one remedial math course; 30 percent of those students were interested in math, science and engineering disciplines.

In 2009 at a local high school, 54 percent of the high school juniors and seniors in the GAP tested out of both remedial math courses; 7 percent tested out of one remedial math course; 37 percent of the students who tested out scored in the 96 and 98 percentile range. More than half of them were interested in pursuing math and science and major courses of study, reading and English.

In the summer '08 pilot program, 36 percent of the students tested out both remedial reading and English courses; 18 percent tested out of one remedial English course.

Summer '09 research report, 44 percent of the high school juniors and seniors tested out both remedial reading and English courses; thereby saving themselves one year of remedial English course work; 25 percent planned to major in English.

These astounding outcomes are based on small pilot programs of 15 to 20 students, but students were selected because they scored at the bottom in all math and English entry test for college. It says that there is a way to close the gap on the worst scorers on these tests so that they all – and the keyword is, *all* – can accomplish, compete and succeed. The Gateway Program has proven this beyond a shadow of a doubt. So how was it done?

Drs'. Hughes and Khatri have written two books, "Color-Blind Teaching: Excellence for Diverse Classrooms," and "American Education Apartheid -- Again?" These two books provide the basis for the pedagogical strategies that are used in the GAP.

The authors stressed, of course, that there are two ingredients for success: Teachers who know what they're doing and students and teachers who are both engaged in the learning process. They establish in Chapter 6 of the "American Education Apartheid -- Again?" how the pedagogy works. Among other things, recognize different knowledge levels of the students (which may in fact, be exactly the reason for pursuing the ideas of multiple "literacies" and multiple intelligences); be sensitive to how one teaches; sustain high expectation levels regardless of cultural diversity; know the content to be taught;

demonstrate energy and enthusiasm; anchor new concepts to familiar experiences; gain the attention of learners before presenting the content; stimulate analogical learning; divide problems into finite steps; structure the subject matter for incremental learning; engage in meaningful practice and repetition (code word, drill); manage classroom; assure equal participation; capitalize on students' good errors; provide sufficient time in the classroom for note taking; minimize deductive learning with beginning students in a discipline; maximize opportunities for inductive learning.[3]

INDUCTIVE/DEDUCTIVE LEARNING

So what anchors the Professors new structure for the delivery of educational content? GAP anchors new concepts to familiar experiences, maximizing inductive learning that moves to deductive learning with beginners in a discipline. The mantra here is to move from the familiar and the simple to the complex:

"...The use of finite steps is not confined to problem solving in the sciences or statistics...The same approach can be used in the social sciences and English. For example, literature is filled with infrequent terms used to convey precise meaning and emotional nuances. Unusual words and phrases are one reason that literature can transport us from the mundane world into more exciting realms. Yet there are steps that often can be used to gain the meaning of an unfamiliar word when a dictionary is not readily at hand." [4]

The turning point it appears for the GAP program is how they're able to train teachers to move across disciplines once they know their own discipline extremely well.

> "…what they need to know is, "what pedagogical principle do I need to use in order to teach my discipline effectively to my students?" "Yet any current effort to teach pedagogy in abstraction or in isolation will only fail as it has in the past. If pedagogy is taught in this way, it will remain out there with no real value."[5]

The value of this new way of training their teachers is the concept of the *new and valuable*. Conceptually it means carrying the teacher into a new discipline to acquire a fresh view of gaining knowledge and using that skill to adapt it to their teaching of their own discipline. Also, Drs. Hughes, Khatri and Brown seek to have the teacher cross walk between disciplines when working in math and physics. They use the GAP method to teach English, grammar and reading, which are both keys to the study of math and science. Consequently, there is a boost in all of the converging disciplines that define the basic skill sets.

What Doctors Hughes and Khatri have done in my estimation is to create a minor revolution, a major miracle, in the presentation, the content, and the innovation around teaching and learning, particularly for students who come from poor and low-income backgrounds and who have not been prepared well for entry into college work. Their groundbreaking work at the University of the District of Columbia should be a model used not only throughout the Thurgood Marshall College System, but also throughout the nation. First, it should be brought to scale beyond the walls of the University of the District of Columbia. It is important to note that this is happening at one of our urban land grant schools. A breakthrough has been made that can absolutely revolutionize how we teach our students and train our faculties to come to grips with closing this gap that is the harbinger of education discussions today.

The total implication of their work is that not only do students improve dramatically, allowing them to pass their math and science courses, but they also improve dramatically in other subjects, particularly in English, literature, and the social sciences simply because these professors have learned how to cross walk learning between the sciences and the social sciences to create a holistic concept for learning.

This program, of course, can be deepened, and widened, and expanded; the kernel of truth involved in how physics and math can create learning in social science and literature is an amazing and astounding one.

CONSILIENCE

Professor E.O. Wilson of Harvard University, an American biologist and Pulitzer Prize winner is world renowned, and in some instances, considered controversial. But his work on Consilience is important to this issue paper. One of the highest priorities of educational reform is teacher quality and closing the education pipeline. In one program, in one HBCU we may have an answer to how this may be done. Professor Wilson of Harvard might call what Professors Khatri, Hughes, and Brown have done, CONSILIENCE - - Professor Wilson is a proponent of the merging of academic disciplines to create a pedagogical set of pathways that go to the heart of learning, and that this learning is characterized by the kind of work that Khatri, Brown, and Hughes are doing. Professor Wilson's idea purports that one can understand the world of knowledge through combining of various disciplines to understand fully the magnitude and the continuum of knowledge itself opens up a whole new vista for how we deliver education to all learners. Because of the tremendous explosion of new knowledge it is certainly an idea worth pursuing.

Frederick M. Hess, in *National Affairs*, Issue 9, Fall 2011, muses as to whether this "Achievement-Gap Mania" has led to educator's policy that has short changed many children. It has narrowed the scope of schooling. It has hallowed out public school support for school reform. It has stifled educational innovation. It has distorted the way we approach educational choice, accountability and reform" (See Appendix G).

SUMMARY

The HBCU network of institutions should build on the work on the GAP program and the work of Professor Wilson at Harvard. This ideal restructuring for curriculum development and pedagogical instruction can be, with great study and care, the hallmark of new education research and application. It might prove to be the ideal way of repositioning how one learns in the 21st century. This is indeed a tremendously important field of study. It would give the HBCU professors a valuable platform upon which to work to create and to envision an academic future that supports the growth and development of not only African-American students, but all students.

NOTES

[1]Ravitch, Diane (2010). The death and life of the great American school system: How testing and choice are undermining education. (pp. 223-224). Basic Books, NY

[2]Ibid (p. 225).

[3]Khatri, Daryao S. & Hughes, Anne O. (2002) American education apartheid - - again?. (p. 82). The Scarecrow Press, Inc., Lanham, Maryland and Oxford

[4]Op. Cit (p. 83).

[5]Ibid (p. 88).

EDUCATION AND BUSINESS:
STRUCTURING THE AFRICAN-AMERICAN STUDENT PIPELINE

A definition of the education pipeline is sought and arguments are made with regard to who is involved and how these actors create the environment out of which workable solutions can be found and implemented. The major options revolve around the thinking of author Thomas Freidman and the desire to create a plan called an Articulation Plan with the Nation's Community Colleges.

Education has become a battleground of theories and ideas. It is awash in money for certain types of reform yet we are still searching for that magic bullet (See Appendix H). Sometimes it's hard to know exactly what the discussion is about. Do we wish to graduate 100 percent of all youth in America from elementary, high school and college? Once graduated, do we then presume that they will all have jobs to participate in society and to create the American dream? Both are most worthwhile ideals. Or, do we wish to develop well rounded individuals who will participate in society as contributing citizens. One would presume the latter.

After the publication of *A Nation at Risk,* in the 1990s, the American business, educational and political communities started on a quest to reform and to revitalize the American public education system because it was not producing students who were competitive in the world arena. Diane Ravitch was a major proponent of the school reform movement a part of the commission that produced *A Nation at Risk.* In her new book, "The Death and Life of the Great American School System: How Testing and Choice are Undermining Education," Dr. Ravitch develops a new narrative regarding American education. She sees the present direction of reform, mainly the privatizing of the nation's public schools by wealthy individuals and their foundations as creating a clear and present danger to the overall system of public education in America.

What we learn from Ms. Ravitch's recantation of the past situation and her observations of the present is that education in America lacks a cohesive, coherent mission that would guide a strong, progressive vision for the entire educational enterprise. It is somewhat disingenuous to attempt to evaluate the present education system since we have no common standards or outcomes other than graduation and testing to measure it by. Young people passing through our system need to know that they can be adequately educated to face what they will meet as job seekers, job developers and job creators.

THE EDUCATION PIPELINE

There are many factors which must be considered to begin the discussion of the education pipeline. Importantly, who is a part of it and why? Most specifically, how do we gauge the participation or the lack of participation of African-Americans?

The American Council on Education (ACE) on its web site provides a very clear understanding of just what the education pipeline is all about in an article entitled *Education Pipeline: Key to Enhancing State's Education Capital.* In this report prepared by Peter T. Ewell, Dennis P. Jones and Patrick J. Kelly of the National Center for Public Policy and Higher Education, they give a very concise and clearly understandable answer to the question of why the educational pipeline is needed. The most compelling fact is that only knowledgeable highly-skilled people in a state's workforce can provide a measure of continuing growth and prosperity for a state. If states are to remain competitive, they must develop an effective educational pipeline. It is the key to the state's educational capital and its financial bottom line.

According to the authors, more states are moving toward adopting education policies that increase the number of students successfully progressing from ninth grade to high school graduation to a four-year degree because the residents holding college degrees are the basis of a state's *educational capital*. High levels of educational capital provide a foundation for a state's economic development and quality of life for its residents.

The pipeline then, as state policymakers view the system, according to the ACE article, should use three primary methods to create greater educational capital. They can do this by creating a high-quality K through 16 system for preparing their students to get a college degree. They can do this by developing and supporting an economy to employ the state's educated residents and then they can attract educated workers who live outside of their state by establishing a strong state economy. The authors also establish particular transition points that they recommend to states regarding the pipeline.

- "Increase **the number of high school graduates**. Develop strategies to improve basic skills; involve parents, business leaders and the community in the education process; and ensure sufficient financial support of low-income districts.
- Improve **college access**. Create tuition policies based on median income and supporting need-based financial aid; build high-capacity, open-entry two-year college systems that encourage transfer; and encourage dual enrollment and advanced placement policies that speed the transition from high school to college.
- Promote **graduation from college**. Set up programs for individual learners; support intensive enrollment in basic coursework in the first year of college; develop schedules based on students' needs; avoid pushing students towards high education debt; and establish transfer polices that retain academic credit."[1]

From this report and the ACE review, the complexities of the education pipeline are very easily understood but maybe not so easily developed. For HBCUs purposes, the pipeline issues revolve around African-American access to public education in our nation. There's been a continual widening achievement gap particularly among young black men and the rest of the nation. This is where the effect of the pipeline issue is most apparent. It is most obvious in high school graduation rates, in college matriculation and graduation rates and in workforce development activity.

And yet, the *Army Times* reports that, "Black College Enrollment in the South Passes a Milestone." The article written by Justin Pope finds, "For the first time ever in the

South, blacks are as well represented on college campuses as they are in the region's population as a whole – something not yet true of the country overall."[2]

The report released by the Southern Regional Educational Board which includes 16 states in the South, states, "black enrollment in college has risen by more than half over the last decade and they now make up 21 percent of college students and 19 percent of the overall population."[3] Yet, "...educators also stressed that the numbers should not obscure the persistent achievement gap affecting blacks both in the South and nationally, in particular, black enrollment rates for college-age students, while improving, still lag well-behind those of whites, as do the graduation rates of black college students."[4] The article goes on to express that there has been tremendous progress, "but don't get me wrong," Board President Dave Spence said, and then added that unless the achievement gaps narrow, "we're going to be in trouble. We're already in trouble but we'll be in more trouble seven or eight years down the road."[5]

The report reflects the reality that many southern blacks are enrolling in college. According to this article, in these states, about 1.1 million black students were enrolled in college in the fall of 2005, 52 percent more than a decade earlier. Today, that figure is relatively unchanged. The article continues stating that, "The increase has come largely from new and expanding public traditionally white colleges and two-year colleges rather than from historically black colleges which for many years shouldered nearly the entire burden on higher education of southern blacks. Many of these schools still exist but their share of black enrollment in the region has slipped from 26 percent to 19 percent over the last decade."[6]

The issue for HBCUs is to reclaim enrollment across the region, where most of our schools are located.

THE HBCU'S EDUCATION PIPELINE

It is for this reason that HBCUs should make it a priority to establish a new invigorated pipeline process that will bring students to participate in America's public black colleges. A company or many companies like CRP, could create the infrastructure that would add business know-how and aggressiveness to create educate outcomes. From the foregoing, it is obvious that there is very little good news in regards to pipeline issues involving African-American students with one exception that African-American women continue to do well while the African-American male continues to lag behind. Everyone agrees that it is in the best interest of the nation if all young people are motivated and prepared to finish school and become contributing citizens. It is also postulated that these young people wish the same thing. How can we make this happen?

The HBCU pipeline could use the broad philosophical outline as discussed in, "The World is Flat," by Thomas Friedman. Not only does he question how we educate our children, but most importantly, he then provides answers to questions that he posed to employers regarding the right stuff for the development of our educational system. First, "the most important ability you can develop in a flat world is the ability to 'learn how to learn'."[7] By that, the author means the ability to absorb what one is taught and to teach one's self new ways of doing things, cultivating flexibility in an era where flexibility will be an absolute necessity.

Secondly, one must have passion and curiosity. The idea is that educational opportunities are limitless in a flat world. What Friedman sees here is the reconfiguration of the pyramid box-style of corporate structure, which of course has framed the education process of the past decades as well. The fact is that this will evolve into a new form and shape so that those graduating from a flat system will have the flexibility to not only participate in their first job but many jobs that will obviously come to them during their work life. He concludes that in a flat world "IQ, intelligence quotient, still matters."[8] But what really counts is the CQ and PQ, -curiosity quotient- and –passion quotient- even more. He postulates the equation is CQ + PQ= IQ. It is his understanding that a kid with passion to learn and curiosity to discover will be far more successful than a high IQ kid in the final analysis.

The third element, is simply put, "you need to like people." That is, you need to be able to manage and interact with individuals of all types in the flat world. People skills will be a necessity.

The fourth element Mr. Friedman discusses is "how to nurture more of your right brain as well as your left brain."[9] According to his thinking, in order to make it in this new environment, our young people will need to have a well-crafted aptitude for "high concept" and "high touch." High concept being the ability to create artistic and emotional beauty, "the ability to create artistic and emotional beauty to detect patterns and opportunities to craft a satisfying narrative and to come up with inventions the world didn't know it was missing. High touch involves the capacity to empathize, to understand the subtleties of human interaction, to find joy in one's self and to elicit it in others and to stretch beyond the quotidian in pursuit of purpose and meaning."[10]

In an article entitled "We Can't Educate our Children Without Educating Ourselves," Bobby Austin makes the point that,

> "the educational system is failing black youngsters. It is estimated that 44 percent of African-Americans are functionally illiterate and 47 percent of all black 17-year olds are functionally illiterate."[11] It is difficult to educate with these liabilities.
>
> An additional issue involves cultural values. "There has been a real disruption in the cultural values in American life. This is not only true for African-American children but for white Americans as well. For an individual to educate himself, he needs to have an idea of what he is educating himself for. And this is even truer for a society as a whole. As a society loses its sense of collective purpose, its children are the first to manifest a loss of individual purpose…in order for a group or a person to be willing to make sacrifices to secure a better future, they must first have to have a shared version of that future…"[12]

This whole issue of culture and shared vision among African-Americans is a critical one and the only way it seems that we they will increase the participation of African-Americans in the education pipeline is to work to make a more concerted effort to develop this shared version. The article that is being referenced here was written for the Congressional Black Caucus magazine, Point of View in 1987, and pointed to a possible shared vision,

"...In the past, at least four visions in turn have organized black America's thoughts, perceptions and achievements. These have been, the vision of Freedom as developed in the Negro spirituals; the vision of Overcoming during the slave trade and in the slave narratives during the Abolition period and Reconstruction; the vision of a New Man America, a new Negro as embodied in the Harlem Renaissance; and, the vision of Civil Rights and equality in the Civil Rights Movement of the 1960s. Each of these large and all-encompassing visions has shaped the actions, politics and education of its perspective era. Each has provided the context on which people, African-Americans, could establish and stake a claim in the development of this nation and consequently, the creation of this culture.

African-Americans need a new shared vision of themselves, a vision that focuses on the context wherein we adults teach and inspire young people to learn. Such a new vision could be concerned with the establishment of the American common culture. Why common culture? Because it is a massively unexplored area that includes all Americans, common culture is the interrelated social facts, myths and arts that lay claim on the total society and search, shape the minds, soul and spirit of that people.

The educational process and function has never stood outside of the social structure and culture. In fact, the educational process and function makes plain for those in the society what the culture is, what it has accomplished, and where it is going.

Our educational system is failing us – all Americans – because those who maintain it are not cognizant of what they must now transmit to their students, not just the basic skills but the socio-civic literacy part of the equation. Students, who by their own apathy fail to buy into the present education system even to their own detriment, are signaling to us a dangerous and massive failure of spirit. Adult leaders, politicians, scholars, teachers, businessmen, clergy, all must be re-educated to the need to create a new dream for our successor generation to share."[13]

If we are to increase the pipeline based on the philosophies that both Friedman and Austin have expressed, there are several things that we must do. One of the most critical is to find a way to enhance the environment in which young African-Americans live and study. One of the most creative that is now evolving rapidly is the pre-K through high school boarding school for students of color.

Just as the charter school movement, which was heavily financed, has spread throughout the United States over the last several decades, the residential school idea has the same potential to develop strong students but with better results. It brings a different approach to the situation. One of the reasons that so many young people cannot make it through the education pipeline is poverty and the environment in which they must live. This is a no-brainer- it is very difficult for these young people to make it through the educational system as it is now established.

Once they return to their homes after the school day, they find it is just not a place for study and reflection. Therefore, the residential schools seem like a very good idea for first breaking the environmental poverty threshold and giving young people a chance and at a successful educational career.

Residential education is of course not new. It has always been in place for the wealthier members of our society and it has also been provided for boys and girls who because of their economic circumstances and/or their home lives could participate. Two of the most outstanding such schools are

St. Benedict's Preparatory School in New Jersey and the Hershey School in Hershey, Pennsylvania. Both of these institutions are exemplary in the work that they do with young people. Residential schooling has been around since the 1700s. But after a White House conference on children in 1919, the deinstitutionalization, as it was called at the time, of removing foster care children from these settings as well as other indigent dependent children, the whole residential school institution began to fade. This movement peaked in the mid-1970s in what was called the warehousing period in favor of what is called family preservation when dealing with parents and children. It is obvious today that as all movements including school reform movement ebb and flow with good intentions, sometimes there are things that should be left in place. Residential charter schools were established, boarding schools are being established so that children have a way to break from the unhealthy environments that they are forced to live in. It is obvious that over the coming years, the residential school movement will certainly have to pick up if the pipeline is really going to establish a footing for many of our young people to start to begin their educational careers.

A new residential school called the Christina Seix Academy, in Trenton, NJ is presently being formed. The Academy is funded by philanthropist Christina Seix. It will be year-round Pre-K through 8th grade primarily serving children living with a single, parent or grandparent or kin beset by acute economic and/or health challenges. It will be co-educational and will embrace the diverse mix of ethnicities. It will be a year-round program and will integrate issues to look closely at residential education as a prime pump to begin the Renaissance of adding more at-risk children into the education pipeline and giving them a fair opportunity to succeed.

Next, we should find ways to implement the CBO-NGO model. Edward E. Gordon in, "Winning the Global Talent Showdown," advocates the establishment of the community-based organizations, non-governmental organizations - - ideal where citizens develop a shared vision on how to create the education to employment system for the 21st century. He relies heavily upon local community action through the CBOs and NGOs to develop what he calls the highly-talented educated workforce. It is his contention that we have the CBOs and NGOs throughout all of our communities in the United States, that the pool of people are available, and include people from labor, education, government, liberal arts education and career institutions, parents and students, incumbent workers, life-long learning employers, and intermediate employers.

What's missing, he says, is

"the pipe that is the structure in between the infrastructure to connect these CBOs and NGOs to nurture and develop the talent that is abundant in the United States. Well, the challenge facing all of us is to create more talented people from those who are now not participating in becoming a part of the American dream."[14]

Of course this kind of cooperative infrastructure building could be accomplished. There is indeed a plank in the land-grant mission of public service that supports our institutions joining forces with community-based organizations and individuals to create and extend the work and education components of the land grant ideal to both rural and urban needs.

REGIONALISM

Overall, the missing piece, or as Gordon would say, the missing "pipe" is an overarching grand scheme to encompass these ideas. It would seem that a regional concept would in fact fit the need. Since a large portion of HBCUs and universities are located in the southern United

States, we therefore believe that a regional concept for the development of a pipeline is necessary so that our colleges can become completely engrossed with helping to find the answers to and the implementation of a pipeline that could have partnerships with both business and government. A regional plan then would offer us the opportunity to focus on best practices, lessons learned and opportunities to carry out this work.

This regional focus would attempt to partner and create a dialogue with organizations like the Appalachian Regional Commission and the Delta Regional Authority, both of whom are working and have for decades to strengthen the capacity of citizens to meet the demands and needs of the present. The education intermediary should encourage the idea that the pipeline would work not only for African-American students but for all students who are poor – and in this region, both black and white. By combining their individual resources, the colleges, business community, state governments and community-based organizations could create a pipeline that could bring lasting sustainable structures to a regional plan. The public colleges, both black and white, could join together to give specific emphasis and attention to the revitalization of this region of the country. A regional focus also would allow for greater funding opportunities and the maximizing of talent, of the tremendous educational resources that are available in this region. With all of the HBCUs schools located here, this could be a major platform for the revitalization and the re-visioning of education in this region and in the nation in general.

If the pipeline is envisioned as a continuum from early childhood through adulthood, then a regional plan is by far the best plan that could be established. It would have Friedman's four themes, Wilson's CBO-NGO model, and the Austin shared vision ideal. It would be a workable plan of action to not just fix the leaks in the educational pipeline but to redefine how we approach the idea of universal education for every child in this nation. Tied to this regional ideal is how to place before young people an end-result. The desire for education must be accompanied with a practical application. The HBCU network has developed two concepts with its 47 institutions that speak to the built-in capacity that this public school-public college alliance has. First, the HBCUs Faculties of Management, which is composed of all 47 schools of business administration, public administration, library and information studies, and resources and environmental studies, have come together in a collaborative way to undertake to prepare a cadre of individuals for the management profession.

This kind of collaboration by itself could add much to a regional focus in creating and implementing the education pipeline; first, because it is organized and prepared and because it works from developmental goals that the member institutions have created. They are: 1) improving the quality of life and income especially for the poor; 2) ensuring good governance; 3) promoting public-private sector growth and employment generation; 4) preserving and promoting cultural heritage and environmental conservation; and 5) achieving rapid economic growth and transformation.

In the same vein, one additional creative aspect of the regional concept would be to establish throughout the cooperative extension/land grant system, a center that would deal directly with the US Department of Labor and businesses throughout the region to create apprenticeships for young men and women, as well as those who are in high school or community college, within the region. Why apprenticeships? It is our thought that apprenticeships offer a long-term opportunity that assures the development of a skill, working under a master craftsperson. It introduces the young person into the field of work but it also offers a way to seal the leaking educational pipeline.

In a paper commissioned for this report, Willie Meaux , a Vice President at the Thurgood Marshall College Fund, writes on apprenticeships,

"...certainly there are ways we can improve U.S. policy and treatment of apprenticeships in the context of education, especially higher education, as the advance skill provided by most apprenticeship opportunities are more likely supported through higher education as technological advances in manufacturing and services require the kind of intensive and specialized curricula that these institutions can turn over. But the need to really modernize the concept of apprenticeship should involve the entire spectrum of K-16 educational opportunity. If we wait for community college as the forum to address literacy, we will have waited far too long, and we'll have significant gaps to overcome and lower successes at accelerating the transfer of skills and technologically savvy worker who emerge from these institutions.

From the Great Depression to the Great Recession, we have had a role for apprenticeships in America that has been diminishing. Perhaps we have been losing manufacturing base over this span of time and saw the apprenticeship as an antiquated way to skill up workforce in these areas. True, manufacturing has been losing ground to services, but the concept of apprenticeship could still help people gain a footing in new professional occupations that may not have benefitted from the model. With 15 million unemployed Americans today, it would seem we might have created mechanisms that direct government programs and cooperative incentives to increase the number of registered apprenticeships well beyond the mere 500,000."

Is it time for Americans to rethink the idea of apprenticeship?

To stimulate and assist industry in developing and improving apprenticeship and other training programs designed to provide the skilled workers needed to compete in a global economy, apprenticeship is a combination of an on-the-job training and related classroom instruction in which workers learn the practical and theoretical aspects of highly skill occupations. Apprenticeship programs in America are sponsored by joint employer and labor groups, individual employees and/or employer associations."[15]

This may be the key to a business-education partnership in sealing the education pipeline and bringing it into full fruition as a workable solution to our workforce development needs and most especially brining young people through the pipeline to real work opportunity. Even if black males are increasingly rare in colleges some headlines have stated, the pipeline if developed in the way that has been suggested in this short paper should be able to create a system that will maintain and support young people as they move toward adulthood in American society.

COMMUNITY COLLEGES

There is one major player in this whole arena that cannot be left out and that is the community college. It would be important for HBCUs to execute an articulation plan between the community colleges in their regions allowing for a greater dialogue between these entities.

Community colleges are critical players in the pipeline. With more than 11.5 million people enrolled, 42 percent full-time, 58 percent part-time; with an average of, 28; and large numbers of minorities – 37 percent-14 percent Black, 16 percent Hispanic. Among its undergraduate students from the United States which is 44 percent of the population, first time freshman compose 40 percent, Native Americans 54 percent, Asian-Pacific Islanders, 45 percent, Blacks 44 percent, Hispanics 51 percent, students; full-time employed full-time 21 percent, and students full-time employed part-time 59 percent. These are the statistics provided by the American Association of Community Colleges – they are proof that community colleges are vital to the post-secondary portion of the pipeline in the United States and for the development of critical skills for the American workforce. (See Appendix I)

It is the obligation of the HBCU community to become more engaged with the community college sector for many reasons. One of the most important is the feeder system potential that could be established between the community college and each of our universities. Generally community college students are low-income; therefore their choices for education may be home-based and low cost.

Consequently, one of the most important factors for the pipeline for African American students will be to create articulation agreements between all of the black colleges and the community colleges in their respective areas. This will then guarantee the opportunity for matriculation of community college graduates into a 4 year curriculum. The 4-year colleges in HBCUs and the 2-year colleges would have to work on curriculum alignments so that students could easily move from AA and AS to BA and BS without restrictions.

"Re-examining the Community College Mission" written by Amaury Nora, College of Education, University of Houston; Houston, Texas and appears on the American Association of Community Colleges Web site, is a historic report that foreshadows studies as recent as 2009 on the history of community colleges. One of the most interesting facts is a look at the follow-up rates of graduation of the huge number of Hispanic and African American students who attend community colleges.

> "Attrition rates of both minorities and non-minorities continue to be a serious problem in most community colleges. Figures on the persistent rates of attrition of community college students reported 10 or 20 years ago (London 1989; Zwerling 1976) are no different today than those in earlier studies. In a national study of minority and non-minorities in both two and four year institutions, attrition rates for all groups remained high. While the attrition rates at certain institutions may imply that students are not dropping out of these in large numbers as in the past, the researchers noted that the withdrawal trend at community colleges is still prevalent specifically with minority student populations. Attrition rates for minority students in two-year colleges are at about 60 percent and in some cases, as high as 80 percent"[16](see Appendix J)

There must be dialogue between four-year colleges and the community college network to establish an articulation plan that would help both institutions to retain their students and bring more community college graduates into the four-year programs of HBCUs institutions. Attention must be placed on the issue of retention for both kinds of institutions. One area we can provide help to community colleges is to share full-time faculty as it is widely believed that a lack of full-time faculty in community colleges contributes to the low attrition rates. Agreement must be established that ensures the pipeline from community colleges to our four year institutions can work seamlessly.

I have excerpted a section from the Education Week report, "The Obama Education Plan," regarding teaching, learning and types of skill development needed in our education system today. It seems the additional factors of soft skill deficiencies are just as important as deficiencies in math and science, some employers believe.

"...As one Arkansas employer said in a focus group, we want somebody who shows up on time, somebody who works hard, and someone who's trainable. James E. Rosenbaum, a sociologist at Northwestern University who's interviewed employers about their workforce needs, says "Employers we interviewed said they were able to redesign jobs around academic-skill deficiencies, but not soft skills deficiencies."

Nearly all jobs, he says, "require basic work habits, such as regular attendance, motivation, and discipline, and our schools are not taking steps to improve students in these areas. Indeed, the opposite may be occurring. If teachers are compelled to focus more on academic skills and test scores, they may devote less attention to soft skills and efforts to improve them."

At least one analysis, by Princeton, New Jersey-based Mathematica Policy Research Inc., suggests that improvements in nonacademic competencies – such as work habits and a belief that success results from hard work rather than luck – may be just as important for improving later earnings and postsecondary success for some students as gains in academic skills.

Using data from the National Educational Longitudinal Survey, or NELS, a federal database that followed a cohort of students from the time they were 8th graders in 1988 until 2000, the study found that for most students, improving one of the nonacademic competencies would have had a larger effect than better math scores on their chances of enrolling in and completing a postsecondary program, with 43 percent benefitting most from an improvement in work habits.

When it came to earning a bachelor's degree, however, improving math scores still had the largest effect for the most students.

In general, the Mathematica study found, students reaped the most benefit from improving in areas where they weak. "Considering individual strengths and weaknesses when deciding which competencies to improve might be a more effective strategy than simply encouraging all students to improve the same competencies," write researchers John Deke and Joshua Haimson.

21ST CENTURY SKILLS

Beyond specific content knowledge and soft skills, researchers increasingly point to a range of applied skills that span academic areas as important for success.

According to Anthony P. Carnevale, an economist and research professor at Georgetown University, individuals who score higher on measures of complex problem-solving, critical thinking, creativity, and fluency with ideas have higher mean earnings in the labor market, across all levels of education.

David T. Conley, a professor of education at the University of Oregon, says that in addition to specific content knowledge, "A range of cognitive and meta-cognitive capabilities, often described as 'habits of mind,' have been consistently and emphatically identified by those who teach entry-level college courses as being as important or more important than any specific content knowledge taught in high school."

Examples include an analysis, interpretation, precision and accuracy, problem-solving, and reasoning, he writes in "Toward a more Comprehensive Conception of College Readiness," a paper prepared for the Seattle-based Bill and Melinda Gates Foundation. Similarly important, he continues, are the attitudes and behavioral attributes that students who succeed in college demonstrate, including study skills, time management, awareness of their own performance, persistence, and the ability to use study groups.

The Harvard University psychologist Howard Gardner, in, "Five Minds for the Future," defines the cognitive abilities that he argues will command a premium in the years ahead.

He describes them as the disciplinary mind (mastering ways of thinking in one or more content disciplines or a professional craft); the synthesizing mind (able to integrate ideas across disciplines and communicate that to others); the creating mind (able to uncover and clarify new problems, questions, and phenomena); the respectful mind (being aware of and appreciating differences among human beings); and the ethical mind (knowing and acting on one's responsibilities as a worker and a citizen).

Unfortunately, Gardner writes, "No one knows precisely how to fashion an education that will yield individuals who are disciplined, synthesizing, creative, respectful, and ethical.

Such skills, moreover, are hard to assess or to insert in content-oriented state high school standards.[17]

"It's easier to get some coalescing around standards with respect to content," says Jones, the Indiana higher education commissioner. "Some of these other concepts – like working in teams, or leadership skills, or communication skills – are harder to quantify and clearly harder to assess. And so I think people recognize their importance, but they're still grappling with how you would actually do it.[18]

More than half the employers surveyed for the Conference Board, for example, said critical thinking and problem-solving were "very important" for successful performance on the job, yet nearly three-quarters rated recent high school graduates as deficient in such skills."[19]

Clearly the need to know what to teach is vital here. Young people may be dropping out because they are too confused. What do I want – teaching to the test or well-rounded individuals or both? And, have we established an agenda to get this result. Where is the seamless education mission for the American education system that includes what our children must learn and how it is integrated into elementary, high school, community college and college? Today they are all separate skyscrapers.

SUMMARY

The regional approach is unique and holistic in its integration of multiple socioeconomic and environmental objectives and offers an opportunity to provide a model to other jurisdictions grappling with educational development issues. The regional approach encapsulates this idea. Practical strategies for achieving sustainable outcomes are possible. The creation of a Community College Articulation Plan could support all stakeholders concerned with the educational enterprise. The education pipeline is the key to all that we do and we should be engaged in policy and solutions in all aspects of the education of American citizens, from kindergarten to workforce development and college opportunities as well as a specific emphasis on the opportunities of regionalism.

NOTES

[1]Ewell, Peter T., Jones, Dennis P. & Kelly, Patrick J. (2004,

April). Policy Alert: Education pipeline: Big
investments, big returns. Retrieved from
http://www.highereducation.org/reports/pipeline/

[2]Pope, Justin (2007, June 28). Army Times: Black college
enrollment in South passes milestone, (¶1) Retrieved
from
http://www.armytimes.com/careers/college/military_blac
k_collegeenrollment_070628/

[3]Ibid (¶3).

[4]Ibid (¶5).

[5]Ibid (¶7).

[6]Ibid (¶10).

[7]Friedman, Thomas (2005). The world is flat: A brief
history of the 21st century. New York: Farra, Straus and
Givoux. (pp. 302-308).

[8]Ibid

[9]Ibid

[10]Ibid

[11]Austin, Bobby (1987, Fall). We can't educate our
children without educating ourselves in point of view.
Congressional Black Caucus Foundation. (pp. 34-35).

[12]Ibid (p. 35).

[13]Ibid (p. 35).

[14]Gordon, Edward E. (2009) Winning the global talent
showdown. California: Bennett-Koehler Publishers. (pp.
178-179).

[15]Meaux, Willie. Commissioned Research Statement.
Director Government Relations. HBCUs.

[16]Nora, Amaury (1988). Re-examining the community
college mission. (p. 7).

[17]The Education Week (2009). The Obama education plan:
An Education Week guide, Jossey-Bass; CA (pp. 186-289)

[18]Deke, John & Haimson, Joshua (2006 September, Vol. 2)
Expanding beyond academics: Who benefits and how?
Mathematica Policy Research. (p. 3)

[19]Garner, Howard (2006) Five minds for the future. Boston,
MA: Harvard Business School Press

THE WORLD HOUSE:
DEVELOPING THURGOOD
MARSHALL'S GLOBAL BRIDGE
BUILDER

The need to provide HBCU institutions and students the opportunity to become bridge builders in today's world is indeed a worthy goal. It is exactly what the modern HBCU education should be concerned with. Dr. King's world house vision is made real in this discussion on the development of World House Fellows.

More than a half century ago, Dr. Martin Luther King, Jr. wrote, "Where Do We Go From Here: Chaos or Community?" In that book his concluding chapter called "The World House", is based on his Nobel Prize lecture, which he delivered at the University of Oslo in December of 1964. The importance of "The World House," is obvious. Dr. King realized that as we came near a particular phase in the Civil Rights Movement, that a new phase would have to emerge if we were to remain a strong and vibrant movement. He knew that a new course of action that led to real and creative ways to engage the African-American community as well as the world community would be needed.

In "The World House", Dr. King makes the following statement (summarized by Carol Bragg). Dr. King calls us to: 1) transcend tribe, race, class, nation and religion to embrace the vision of a World House; 2) eradicate at home and globally the triple evils of racism, poverty and militarism; 3) curb excessive militarism and shift from a thing-oriented society to a people-oriented society; and, 4) resist social injustice and resolve conflicts in the spirit of love embodied in the philosophy and methods of non-violence.

He advocates a Marshall plan to eradicate global poverty, to provide a living wage and a guaranteed minimum annual income for every American family. He urged the United Nations to experiment with the use of non-violent direct action in international conflicts. The final paragraph warns of the fierce urgency of now and cautions that this may be the last chance to choose between chaos and community.

The importance of this statement by Dr. King is of course visionary. His prophetic words, again from, "Where Do We Go From Here: Chaos or Community?," "Therefore, I suggest that the philosophy and strategy of non-violence become immediately subject for study and for serious experimentation in every field of human conflict, by no means excluding the relationships between nations." He went on to say that the whole "World House" must be "involved in a revolution of values."[1]

To him these values had to support a culture and a world of justice and principles which lead to peace. It is obvious that the way to bring Dr. King's World House to reality is to embed them within a mission and a vision which guides the education process in some form. Education is nothing more than the harnessing of ideas to propel the individual toward actions that make for a better life, a better world and better understanding of why we are who we are and why we do what we do.

In order to make sacrifices for education or for learning of any type, one must have a very good idea as to why it is being done. If a society is losing a collective purpose – as we seem to be in the United States – we will have trouble in our educational process because it is difficult to know what to teach, how to teach it and why one is preparing to learn.

Many young people today feel they are prevented from succeeding or even participating in American society. And it may be because without a vision, one becomes disoriented as to what the purpose of life is. They succumb to satisfying themselves through an endless series of immediate desires and endless forays and destructive behavior. It's important that young men and women in the HBCU'S network be able to create and own a vision larger than themselves. And in this vision, all of the world could participate.

It seems that it would be more than appropriate to advance the cause of the World House as a centralizing force to organize the vision and creativity of the young men and women in the America's HBCU network. In doing so they will clearly understand, if they are prepared, they can lead the world to peace and justice – but preparation requires education. The education that we are proposing would be one that would equip them for this task.

LEADERS OF THOUGHT AND CULTURE

It is certainly true that education is the most powerful force for change. It is the guiding structure for the development of leadership in our nation. One of the most powerful intellectual leaders of our time has been Dr.

W.E.B. Du Bois. Dr. Du Bois called powerful African American leaders, "leaders of thought and missionaries of culture." If we at HBCUs can create a cadre of leaders of thought and missionaries of culture, we will have implemented the beginning process of Dr. King's World House. The World House, as he called it, was the inheritance that we as human beings have received as a fact of being born on this planet. The World House is given to us as an inheritance; our task is to learn how to live together in it. We are at this point having a very difficult time doing this. It calls upon an exceptional group of people to bring this to reality.

In order to be the innovative system that HBCUs desire, there are certain preconditions that must be met. In a study carried out by Anthony F.C. Wallace, in the *Social Context of Innovation,* he outlines the necessary characteristics that institutions must have in order to host and incubate innovation: 1) the institution must have survived two or more generations; 2) the institution must have access to resources – money, land, physical plant, skilled labor; and 3) the institution must regard the support of innovation as part of its own liability, that is, it must invest in that innovation. The only caveat that should be added here, is that in today's warp speed world, waiting two generations for innovation is not feasible even if desirable. He also lists two general ideas that must be met. And that is that the technology is seen as contributing to social progress and that the social structure be porous, permitting people from all stations of life – from innovative artisans to entrepreneurs to the religious – to participate in the creative process.[2]

Certainly, HBCUs qualify as such as entity but needs to increase in each area so that it can be the innovator that it proposes or seeks to be. The basis for its future endeavors lies within this ideal and is based in many ways on the fact that robust dialogue and conversation would be carried on with its 47 institutions to engage them in the creation of this World House vision that would then form a process for future development sustainability.

In the renowned book, "The World is Flat," by Thomas L. Friedman, he makes this statement which is apropos for the establishment of a global vision for education. He states, "In the future, how we educate our children may prove to be more important than how much we educate them,"[3] It is this particular type of thinking that is guiding those scholars, entrepreneurs and industries that are making cutting-edge forays into a new world of innovation, invention and insightfulness. So how we learn can become the mantra for how we implement and facilitate the World House as a vision for learning.

In many ways, the public black college network has always operated in this fashion. For instance, George Washington Carver was what one might call a *bridge builder*. In the same sense, the man for whom the fund is named, Chief Justice Thurgood Marshall also operated in this fashion. He stated, "The battle for racial and economic justice is not yet won. Indeed, it is has barely begun. The legal system can force open doors and sometimes knock down walls but it cannot build bridges. That job belongs to me, to you, to all of us. Take a chance when you knock down the fences that divide. Tear apart the walls that imprison. Reach out, for freedom lies just on the other side." Justice Marshall understood that bridge builders would be those people who would create the pathways over which the true freedom and democratic process and democracy and prosperity would come.

George Washington Carver was the historic epitome of this bridge builder in the land-grant tradition. Carver was asked to come to Tuskegee by the famed Booker T. Washington; he went there as the first director of the Agricultural Experiment Station. And while there, he was a tremendous pioneer, developing information bulletins for local farmers, creating recipes with different vegetable crops and most importantly, creating an innovative spirit from which Carver developed 120 different uses for the sweet potato and more than 300 products from the peanut. He was a visionary and stabilizing force in the rural segregated South.

But one of the most important things that he and Washington did was to create the first movable school in the South. It was a mule-drawn wagon stuffed with educational materials and it traveled from farm to farm, demonstrating his new agricultural techniques. Carver designed the wagon, but it was the students of Tuskegee who built it. That little wagon went to whoever needed assistance. Black and white alike! Everyone was a beneficiary of the educational process created by Carver and Washington. Here is tangible reality of bridge builders in the spirit of the land-grant tradition, in the same way that Thurgood Marshall called for in the arena of Civil Rights and social justice.

At Fisk University, Dr. Charles S. Johnson developed and led the Race Relations institute which was a seminal platform for building dialogue between white and black social scientist as well as inter-racial audiences. The following excerpt from "Intelligent and Effective Directions, the Fisk University Race Relations Institute and the Struggle for Civil Rights 1994-1969," by Katrina M. Sanders, reveals the way in which Dr. Johnson's bridge building at a HBCU laid the foundation for Interracial dialogue.

THE FISK UNIVERSITY RACE RELATIONS INSTITUTE

"When the RRI opened its doors on July 3, 1944, it was armed with noted professors of anthropology, sociology, economics, and education as well as white and black professional workers and students from various fields including social welfare, labor, religion, education, industry, and government. Although the RRI was the first of its kind in the South, the experimental project was not a new concept for Johnson. It was grounded in a "lineal and logical outgrowth of research and educational work" that had been ongoing for many years at Fisk's Department of Sociology and Anthropology and the Social Science Institute and similar work done for Swarthmore College in Swarthmore, Pennsylvania, during the summer months from 1933 to 1938....

...Johnson felt that because racial tensions were brewing across the country, America needed a unified knowledge of the status of racial and cultural minority groups. Basically concerned with competition between groups and accommodation of minority groups, Johnson utilized Park's frame of reference to shape the general theoretical structure of the Fisk Institute. The frame of reference would accommodate training and research and deal with the distinctive character of national cultures, migrations, statuses of minority and dependent groups in culturally advanced as well as culturally backward areas, and the effects of local customs and social and political restrictions as barriers to effective intergroup relations. Johnson believed that a separate black culture could not exist in the United States even though the thought may have appealed to many blacks. The above frame of reference was useful because as Johnson saw it, the goal for blacks was equal opportunity and assimilation.

The RRI's foundation in a research-based perspective for social action can first be seen in its initial incorporation into the framework of Fisk University as a nonprofit organization. ...The Institute's underlying belief that social change could be fostered by using research to appeal to the morality of the dominant white culture can also be seen in statements and announcements made about the program. In a 24 June 1964 article announcing the start of the '64 program, Institute director Herman H. Long stated that the program's purpose was to: help preserve the integrity of law, to substitute reason for hysteria, to maintain communications between groups and to pursue the steady course of justice founded on religious conviction....

The 1965 program also points out the underlying belief in morality:

...sought to look beyond the significant events in the current racial scene to see their implications for a society which cherishes the political ideals of the Declaration of Independence and the religious ideals of the Judeo-Christian tradition.

The Institute's format also indicates its commitment to a research-based agenda for social change. Patrick Gilpin shares that Johnson first saw the RRI as a type of professional conference where some 30 persons would read papers and facilitate discussions; however, because Johnson received such favorable and enthusiastic feedback to his invitations, he decided to expand the program. To do this, Johnson organized the RRI into three major operating sections. The first section concentrated on training in the social sciences. Here, provisions were made to ensure that undergraduate and graduate students would be a part of the cooperative program. Advanced graduates who already had a Master's degree were encouraged to spend a year at the Institute as research fellows. This year was spent gaining training and research experience and working on a doctoral dissertation under the supervision of the staff. Those graduate students without Master's would receive Training Fellowships that would enable them to conduct research on various minority group relationships with the United States and abroad. This work would culminate in a Master's theses. Undergraduate students would be encouraged to enter the field through tuition waivers and honor's courses. This coordinated approach was intended to provide an extensive body of knowledge in the field of race relations and a reservoir of trained personnel.

The second major operating section focused on research in the social sciences. Here, current research was exchanged and provided to participants of the Institute. The third major operating section of the RRI concerned social action. Methods and techniques in dealing with racial tensions as well as community planning were covered in this section. This section was also responsible for the Race Relations Field staff, the Institute program, the Fisk University Social Center, and the *Monthly Summary of Trends and Events in Race Relations*. ...

> Key to the RRI's conception was the belief that while technological advances in trade, communication, and transportation contributed to race and culture consciousness throughout the world, America, or the "Great Society," lacked the "social and moral unity" which Institute organizers felt could only come through "intelligent direction by specialists trained in the social science of human relations."[4]

The consequences of a vision like that of the World House, encompasses the thoughts of these historic figures and brings us full circle to an old idea and a new reality – innovation. The innovative spirit must propel Dr. King's, "fierce urgency of now," as the contextual framework that is both a land-grand historical marker and a Civil Rights agenda item. The question now becomes, how do we implement this vision?

WORLD HOUSE FELLOWS

The beginning phase of this program should include a year-long structured dialogue between the 47 institutions that are a part of the Thurgood Marshall network. That dialogue would define the tools that would be needed to implement this vision, a concrete and yet open structure of what this vision would look and feel like, including a curriculum and the tools for bringing that curriculum to the classroom, as well as to the community, and the outcomes and skills that individual students would acquire as a part of this new academic learning process.

For instance, there are at least two International Organizations that should be engaged in the development of the World House. One is the Collegium of African-American Research scholars who are located in Europe. These groups of scholars who work in European universities devote their time and research attention to the study of African-American life and culture and, consequently, would make great partners as they stretch our study and concentration from the U.S. to all of Europe and the world.

And secondly, is an organization run by Dr. Leo Cherry, the African Scientific Institute, which is a worldwide collaborative organization of science and technology scholars.

World House Scholars would become engaged in global science and technology dialogues in America, Africa and Europe. They would be exposed to a broad vision that encourages their participation as global actors. For both the Collegium and the Institute (and other national and international partners), they would become the bridge builders between their universities and their communities and those throughout the world represented by these two organizations. Conferences, lectures, research and the dissemination of reports in and around the participation of our students in world forums and as persons engaged in international affairs would be the outcome of this program.

Our students would become citizen diplomats, in effect. *Citizen Diplomacy* was developed and written by Michael Shuman and Gale Warner. They make the following observations regarding citizen diplomats.

"The term, "citizen diplomats", is appropriate because – many American citizens who travel throughout the world – are deliberately trying to improve nation-to-nation relations and reduce the risks of war – the central task of diplomacy.

Hans Morgenthau, one of America's foremost international relations scholars, has defined diplomacy as the method government's use for "establishing the preconditions for permanent peace." Traditional diplomats serve as the nations' legal representatives who negotiate and enter treaties; they serve as symbolic representatives who can show respect for other nations' diplomats, through lavish ceremonies and parties and they serve as the nerve center of foreign policy...the outlying fibers maintain the two-way traffic between the home country and the outside world.

The citizen diplomat serves analogous functions. While they cannot undertake the quest for a "permanent peace" on behalf of the United States government, they can claim to represent smaller chunks of America – churches, businesses, civic groups, local governments or of Americans of like mind. On behalf of these constituents, the citizen diplomats often negotiate and enter into agreements...they demonstrate their respect and goodwill...and they maintain their own two-way traffic of information and impressions by reporting home on their view of events...

In short, while traditional diplomats serve as conduits between America and (the world), citizen diplomats serve as conduits between the American and (worlds people) people. Yet

citizen diplomats affect both nations, leaders as well. Sometimes
they do this by working alongside the traditional diplomats. More
often, however, they affect political context in which leaders
operate by spreading information and forming people-to-people
relationships."[5]

There are three strategies that citizen diplomats can be
identified with (a) influencing leaders; (b) spreading
information; and (c) forming relationships.

INNOVATION AND INVENTION

The search for meaning and reality must always be at the
very forefront of the educational enterprise. These then
must become the watch words of this generation of leaders
within the Public Black College Network. The African-
American has a rich history and tradition of scholars and
leaders and thinkers who not only envision for themselves
but for the world in general. The World House is no
exception. It is a way to create a new guiding principle as it
works parallel to the general educational enterprise of post-
secondary education in the African-American college
network.

SUMMARY

The prospect of global citizenship as an outcome of this vision is centered in the development of fellowships that would be created for students in their last two years of college and through years after their graduation. This particular fellowship would grow out of a course of study over a period of a year in which HBCUs students and faculty and staff would have been engaged in a general collaborative work to find ways to create peace and understanding not only at home but abroad. They would be prepared to work in international organizations and to be volunteers in such organizations. The list could go on and on as we develop and create this World House fellowship in which these students would have the privilege of participating. The ideal would be that they would give two years of their lives in support of the ideals of Thurgood Marshall, W. E. B. Du Bois and Martin Luther King as global citizens.

NOTES

[1]King, Martin L. (1968) Where do we go from here: Chaos or community? Boston, MA: Beacon Press

[2]Wallace, Anthony F. C. (1982, October). The social context of innovation. Anthony F.C. Wallace Papers American Philosophical Society. Princeton, NJ: Princeton University Press

[3]Friedman, Thomas. (Revised 2006). The world is flat: A brief history of the 21st century. New York: Farra, Straus and Givoux. (p. 302).

[4]Saunders, Katrina M. (2005) Intelligent and effective directions: The Fisk university race relations institute and the struggle for civil rights 1944-1969. NY: Peter Lang Publishing. (p .37-39)

[5]Gale Warner and Michael Shuman, Citizen Diplomats; Pathfinders in Soviet-American Relations and How You Can Join. Continuum, NY; 1987, pp. 4-5

THURGOOD MARSHALL
COLLEGE FUND:
UNIVERSITIES AND THE BUILDING
OF SUSTAINABLE COMMUNITIES

The building of sustainable communities which can undergird economic growth and reweave the social fabric of community life is a part of the land grant tradition. This can be done by creating the education/social infrastructure, a web portal. This portal would be a *super university*, an online consolidation of the holdings and offerings of the HBCU'S institutions, creating the foundation and providing the tools and programs to support sustainability.

We sometimes feel safe in our assumptions regarding the many complex issues affecting the African-American family and its community. We are under the impression that we are talking about that one-fourth of this population which struggles to make ends meet.

It has, however, come to light over the past several years that the black working and middle-class is in a state of stagnation. The decline of African-Americans in union and manufacturing jobs from 1997 to 2006 (one of the effects of globalization) has certainly played a pivotal role. An article by John Schmidt and Ben Zippert discusses this downturn of African-American participation in unions and manufacturing. These jobs have been a major platform from which families reach and retain working and middle-class status. Zippert and Schmidt reason that the decline in unionization rates among African-Americans is related specifically to the decline of the U.S. manufacturing base, particularly the automotive industry where so many working class African Americans worked. This is important to note because it is a significant problem that arises when men and women, who rely completely upon their job for their economic status and for the well-being of their children, lose their jobs and are out of work for an extended period of time.

Additionally, Douglas J. Besharov at the University of Maryland made the economic stagnation of the black middle-class the center piece of his testimony before the U.S. Commission on Civil Rights in 2006. According to the author, the black middle-class was growing in absolute numbers, but so were their general population numbers. Consequently, the percentage of growth has remained flat. This is a very important because you wish to see not just the absolute numbers go up, but the percentage of people moving into and expanding the black middle-class growing and developing. The shocking conclusion that the author comes to as one reason for this stagnation is due to the differences in educational attainment between whites and blacks today. That is, the black middle-class is not growing because of the extremely high dropout rates and low college graduation rates of black college students compared to whites.

In a 2007 Washington Post article, *Middle Class Dream Eludes African American Families,* Michael Fletcher writes,

"nearly half of African Americans born to middle-income parents in the late 1960s plunged into poverty or near-poverty as adults, according to a new study – a perplexing finding that analysts say highlights the fragile nature of middle-class life for many African Americans. Overall, family incomes have risen for both blacks and whites over the past three decades. But in a society where the privilege of class and income most often perpetuate themselves from generation to generation, black Americans have had more difficulty than whites in transmitting those benefits to their children.

Forty-five percent of black children whose parents were solidly middle-class in 1968 – a stratum of medium income of $55,600 in inflated-adjusted dollars – grew up to be among the lowest fifth of the nation's earners, with a median income of $23,100. Only 16 percent of whites experienced similar downward mobility. At the same time, 48 percent of black children whose parents were in an economic bracket with a median family income of $41,700 sank into the lowest income group."[1]

This troubling picture of black economic evolution is contained in a package of three reports being released today by the Pew Charitable Trusts that test the vitality of the American dream. Using a nationally representative data source that for nearly four decades has tracked people who were children in 1968, researchers attempted to answer two questions: Do Americans generally advance beyond their parents in terms of income? How much of that is affected by race and gender?

HBCU GOAL

Indeed these are worthy research questions that must be answered. In the meanwhile, it is incumbent upon HBCUs to search for immediate and short-term goals to incubate a renaissance of social cohesion and stability where job creation and educational pursuits can be brought together through the network of our 47 public educational institutions.

The need for actions to sustain fragile communities is apparent. Based on available research and analysis, the key for both maintaining economic gains and passing them to future generations is, of course, is education. The gravity of this situation is tied to community building. It is in community where individuals prepare for living, absorb their values, act out their modes of conduct and live their dreams, while establishing the goals and ideals that they will seek to achieve. It is the lived culture, whether it is in a rural or urban community.

The important matter of community building must be a priority for the nation's public black colleges. The implicit ideals in community building form the basis for why we educate ourselves. A truly innovative approach to redevelopment would require public black colleges to embed these ideals in their academic and outreach agendas. The issue here is to find ways to reconnect families and individuals to productive life choices. The approach must be crafted in ways that would support and establish a stabilizing platform designed to revitalize rural and urban communities and to inform individuals and families to connect with greater opportunities educationally and economically.

The means by which this can be done is the education social infrastructure. This infrastructure is a web-based portal. It would connect people with resources, programs, courses of study and entrepreneurial activities in multiple ways. It would support communities in crafting long term and short term interventions, multiple solutions to specific issues and bring to their attention lessons learned, best practices, personal mentors, support systems and grassroots organizations. Its most important effect would be to provide a multiplicity of educational activities that would be drawn from the combined academic offering of the HBCU institutions. This would support a super university construct from which a person could draw multiple learning opportunities. This super university construct would connect governments, local, national and international, religious institutions, social net agencies, youth development centers, arts and humanities centers and a plethora of entrepreneurial, incubator opportunities.

This infrastructure would be the organizing principle around which major collaborative efforts could be facilitated by government, religious organizations, private agencies and the philanthropic world.

Susan Boyd of Concerned Inc., says, a sustainable community "resembles a living system, in which all resources, human, cultural, natural and economic are interdependent and draw strength from each other." This is an avenue that must be established if we are to bring creativity and innovation and therefore sustainability back to these communities.

FATHERS OF THE INTERNET

Fathers of the Internet, Robert E. Kahn, Chairman and CEO and president of the Corporation for Research Initiatives, and Vincent Surf, senior vice president of technology strategy for MCI, are known as the fathers of the Internet. Surf is the co-designer of what is called the TCP-IP protocols and the architecture of the Internet. These two gentlemen worked as collaborators in the 1970s – creating the protocols, architecture, and structure which would eventually lead to the Internet that we use today. Working with the government and other private sources, these gentlemen created a whole new world which now influences how we live our lives. But what is key about this invention is the use of the discipline and symbols of "architecture." The creative conceptualizations and connectivity of various concepts, ideas and models that they call protocols, when put together, provide the entrance into an entirely new way of conceiving how we deliver and receive data. This allows us to reinvent how we use data to conceive and shape ideas, develop new jobs, form new businesses and invent new lifestyles. This is what is needed in the whole social realignment for families in fragile communities. The same intensity of innovation, research and development dollars could be found to create social architectural teams within the black college networks to work with each of their communities to build this dynamic architectural grid.

Using the example of the fathers of the Internet, it may be that the following could be accomplished: a technology hub could be developed that would include several states in which one university would be the major center per state or region. There could probably be an establishment of a network of broadband systems that would bind the 25 colleges and universities. An example of this has already taken place at Georgia Tech, where they are building out broadband technology as a unit within the university system. The building of this technology grid would support homes, schools, community organizations and their workers, and would provide information, education, labs for creative software development, and the creation of small, community-based, and home-based businesses. Finally, part of the hubs would include a center for sustainable development within each of the communities where community stakeholders, such as community-based and grass-roots organizations would collaborate with the university and other stakeholders to undergird the development of the community itself.

MARSHALL DU BOIS UNIVERSITY COLLEGES

One thing that should be looked at would be the development of a container system that would be called the Marshall Du Bois University Colleges. These self-contained units would reside in between the universities and the communities. They could physically be on the university campus or they could have a building in the community but more than likely they would be a virtual presence. The point is that they would not interfere with the normal operations of the schools, but would allow for collaboration using faculty and staff as a part of their manning of these college constructs, virtual or actual. We will call them colleges because we want them to be known as educational centers for the community.

Knowing that the only way to remove people from poverty is education, we're going to have to have a bold, new track that pulls people in who need to do a General Education Diploma (GED). This would be a place to do it, instead of the university, if the university setting is sometimes too frightening. The idea is to build this middle road that would run throughout the Thurgood Marshall College Fund Network that would be an intersecting point for the community and the colleges to come together and work to change the educational and economic outcomes of the children and adults in these communities. Also, it would remain a major avenue of the land grant tradition of the universities, focusing on teaching research and service as applied community ideals.

The Marshall Du Bois University Colleges would have local, national and international ramifications. There are at least five schools that have developed in their land grant traditions major concepts of delivery of research and service that could be applied throughout this system and replicated with success. They are the University of Maryland-Eastern Shore, Kentucky State, Florida A&M University, Tuskegee University, North Carolina A&T, Medgar Evers College, and City University of New York.

PUBLIC BLACK COLLEGES AS CREATIVE INDICATORS

Creativity can be seen in the development of its orchid laboratory and nursery in Prince Anne County using a grower's greenhouse to develop the process. President

Thelma Thompson of Maryland Eastern Shore University made the point well when she received a major award from NASULGC for the university's creativity. This quote appears on the University's web site, "By focusing on the value of land grant universities' engagement with their communities, this NASULGC award encourages our continuing effort at UM-ES to enhance the well-being of the citizens of Maryland, particularly here on the Eastern Shore." She goes on to say that a substantial proportion of greenhouse growers' network members are women, first time farmers, or both. One of the workers observed that interest has been growing, and the greenhouse growers' network has grown in eight years from a few to over 40 growers. FARMS (Farmer Access to Regional Markets) is an agricultural supply change model developed by the Rural Development Center at UMES and is responsible for the creation of the greenhouse growers' network. President Thompson and her team see that this model shows promise of enabling lower-income families to become vegetable growers. This is a basic example of what could be accomplished. This project has already spread to Jamaica, and its potential for growth and development throughout the small islands and small nations of the world is unlimited. And yet its focus is very much a local one as well that involves local people in developing community around a growth industry.

This is just one example of many, including the Florida A&M University research activities around Parkinson's disease, which is related to its College of Pharmacy. The work involves partnering with a bio pharmaceutical company to create compounds to treat the disease. A project like this could be an enthralling museum exhibit throughout all of the university colleges for young people to come, view and experiment with the research on groundbreaking, cutting-edge solutions to treating disease that in fact may be in their own families. This would be a fantastic way to learn and to participate in learning.

The Joint School of Nano Science and Nano Engineering created by North Carolina A&T and the UMCG, with the support of the University of North Carolina system, the North Carolina General Assembly, and the Greensboro/Triad Community could bring to the world's attention, the groundbreaking nature of research on public black college campuses while providing opportunities for young scholars to be introduced to new career opportunities.

Tuskegee, on the other hand, is following the legacy of heritage in its National Center for Bioethics Research and Health Care. Relating back to the infamous syphilis studies, they have built on this negative legacy to create the nation's first bioethics center devoted to engaging the sciences, humanities, law, and religious faith in the exploration of the core moral issues which underlie research and medical treatment of African-Americans and other underserved people.

This is both a community of learning and work-related program, but its worldwide implications – worldwide impacts are obvious. Again, the opportunities exist to share these innovations across the HBCU'S superstructure.

At Kentucky State, the limits are being pushed in Distance Learning, a key node in the grid for building an education social infrastructure. Quoting from their annual report of 2008 and 2009, "Many students from all over the United States and some foreign countries have become involved in KSU's aquaculture program by taking online Internet courses. During the reporting period, online fish genetics was taught by Dr. Darius Gomelsky in the fall semester of 2009 with nine students in seven U.S. states and one foreign nation."

Since offering (their) first Internet course in 1992, the division has had a total of 217 online students in 37 U.S. states and 17 countries, an absolute example of what can happen from the very local to the global. It is from this kind of built in capacity that the education/social infrastructure will emerge.

At the Medgar Evers College in the City University of New York, the new Leadership Center for Urban Solutions is leading a new discourse with the community. At this center, ex-inmates, researchers and lobbyists, created a think tank to bring about balance in criminal justice policy making. Together those who have committed crimes, the communities in which they live, and policy makers engage in creating new policies. The most important facet of this program, according to an article that appears in *Diverse* magazine February 18, 2010, is the fact that policy is made with the formally incarcerated as an essential part of that discussion.

This is a groundbreaking idea. It is one which brings the community and the college into very close contact in ways that allow the college to be a supporter as well as a facilitator in the growth and the development of the men and women and their families who have been involved in the criminal justice system.

Each of these programs has the potential for local, national, and global facets. They are in the mode of George Washington Carver's posture of helping others, no matter their color or income, just focusing on the exploration of new ideas, new products, and innovative outcomes. The work is at the very heart of the public land grant tradition. In the final analysis, people want solutions to problems that work, and it does not matter the color of the skin, but more the content of the character and the consequences in the overall solution to the problem.

SUMMARY

Communities can be rewoven if the right protocols and insights are brought together. The elements for this work are already in place for us to begin to collaborate. The establishment of a series of protocols which weave together technology, public black colleges' best practices inside a self-contained unit called the Marshall Du Bois University College could be the platform for supporting sustainable communities. These communities have the power to incubate new ideas and provide structures for multi-generational job development, workforce skills development and entrepreneurial endeavors. For HBCUs, this effort would create a super university technology infrastructure from which persons in our network as well as those nationally and internationally could participate.

NOTES

[1]Fletcher, Michael (2007, November 13). Middle class dream eludes African American families. *The Washington Post.* Retrieved from http://www.washingtonpost.com/wp-dyn/content/article/2007/11/12/AR2007111201711.html

RACE IN THE 21ST CENTURY:

ITS STUDY AND APPLICATION FOR

HISTORICALLY BLACK COLLEGES

Race and race relations have become openly unpleasant in the last several years. How can the issues of race be reframed in light of the many revolutionary discoveries in the past decade involving DNA and the steady stream of archaeological findings placing the origin of mankind in Africa? It would appear that a new frame regarding race could be developed. This paper attempts to address this question.

When we look at the Matterhorn, one thought comes to mind. It possesses tremendous beauty, trajectory and force. Its formation really is a metaphor for the race confrontation that has taken place over the last 500 years. More than two million years ago when Pangaea, the one continent, broke into several pieces forming the present-day continents, the land masses Laurasia containing Europe and Gondwana containing Africa, moved toward one another forming what is now the Matterhorn.

Interestingly enough, as they pushed towards one another, Europe pushed beneath the African platelet causing it to rise above the European platelet. This upward push caused the majestic peak now called – the Matterhorn. As sight such as this, and with such an interesting geological background, certainly makes for great conversation, but it could also represent an idea that symbolizes the chaotic situation that continues to exist in the United States around ideas of race. This is not a pretty picture. Race here in the 21st century continues to occupy center stage in almost every domestic issue. Rather than a majestic symbol of different groups working toward peace and reconciliation, it is a quagmire of who is inferior and superior and who is on top and who is at the bottom. There is very little about the meeting of these two groups in America that can be called majestic. Even though some examples do exist, we seldom talk about our commonalities but rather our differences.

The idea which floated through the media after the election of President Obama was that we had reached a post-racial environment in the United States. Of course, nothing could have been further from the truth. Because there is so much more that we need to do and say in order to understand the deep racial environment in which we all live. Race is very much a part of defining the social, economic and political forces around our school systems, our pipeline issues, our governance issues, issues of equal opportunity, and how we define ourselves. Why is this so? Because the west has constructed a frame for viewing the world and the frame has defined various people around the world as inferior based on color and hair texture and they attributed role signs of various types to define them. This frame places whites at the top. But this is not the whole story, according to sociologist Herbert Blumer,

> "Positive images of white Americans do not stand alone. In the white mind, as in white actions, images of and feelings about the white self and white society are often associated with a range of images and feelings about the racial 'others'."[1]

Certainly members of the dominant racial group differ significantly in the way that they think about and act towards these racial others. Some may be, as Blumer suggests, openly hostile, while others may have

> "charitable, protective feelings marked by a sense of piety and tinctured by benevolence. Others may be condescending and reflect mild contempt, and others may be disposed to politeness and considerateness with no feeling of truculence. Yet others...may be strongly anti-racist in their views of dispositions.

'Over several centuries, whites have constructed an array of sincere fictions about the race of others as with sincere fictions about the white self. Fictional representations of racial outcomes often prevent individuals from seeing or seeing clearly that their society is pervaded by widespread racial prejudice and discrimination. The character of the representations often shifts over time.

'Increasingly, survey researchers generally report a steady decline in traditional anti-black stereotyping and prejudice among whites over the last century. However, although whites' expressions of traditional prejudices and stereotypes in the public arenas are, to survey researchers, have declined in number, this does not mean that anti-black stereotypes, sentiments, and discrimination are now of little consequence in the United States. Numerous researchers have noted the contemporary forms and emphasis of attitudinal expression are often different from the traditional racial stereotypes and prejudices expressed by whites, particularly those articulated prior to the 1960s Civil Rights Movement."[2]

After the historic election of President Obama to be the 44th president of the United States, the dialogue on race and ethnicity in America was changed. The election also changed the concept of leadership in American life. It brought to the forefront the issue of how one defines oneself in a multiracial society. The predominant black/white dichotomy seems to be weakening in favor of the content of character as opposed to the color of one's skin. Media commentators continue to refer to it as post racial. Other Americans have claimed Obama's "biracial" heritage, claiming he belongs to this group or the other.

No matter what you say or where you stand on the issue, the fact is now we are in open discussion. We are engaged in open discussion regarding ideas that just a few short years ago would not have been taken seriously by the general public. The air is filled with the idea of change throughout America. It would be important for all Americans to begin to look at this new set of ideas, perspectives, and assumptions to determine where we each fit now. The old models and narratives may possibly be outmoded, and we must ask, how does this all affect me, and, most importantly, who is defining the moment.

Conceptually, the public black colleges of America should stand ready to fulfill Dr. Martin Luther King, Jr.'s comprehensive World House plan. In effect, the new narrative in the post-election dialogue is really the fact that now individuals must complete the process of change in America. We need a new definition of who that leadership will be and who and what is the new American. It can and must be found and defined in many different ways, and America's public black colleges must be one of those forums through which these discussions take place.

DIFFICULT DIALOGUES

The phrase "difficult dialogues" was coined by Dr. Beverly Guy Shefthall, a professor at Spelman College, to capture the ongoing debates within America's higher education community. How do we know or sense the need for such dialogues? We sense this need because as a nation we are in search of our souls. In the nineteenth century, Ralph Waldo Emerson defined both soul and culture in his essays. In our attempt to define our culture, which is at the root of all of our discussions, there's much, possibly too much, from which to choose. In general, it also can be defined either as a biological phenomenon, a social phenomenon, or even an economic phenomenon.

The deconstruction of race dialogue, began in 1854, when Frederick Douglass pinned an address called, "The Claims of the Negro Etymologically Considered." And in it, Douglass, who was both a man of color and an abolitionist, raised and answered that same question regarding the black man. He posed to his audience and the world whether the Negro was a man...

"A respectable public journal published in Richmond, Virginia bases its whole defense of the slave system upon the denial of the Negro's manhood. "The white peasant is free, and if he is a man of will and intellect can rise in the scale of society, or at least his offspring may. He is not deprived by law of those "inalienable rights," "liberty and the pursuit of happiness," by the use of it. But here is the essence of slavery, that we do declare the Negro destitute of these powers. We bind him by law to the condition of a laboring peasant, forever, without his consent, we bind his posterity after him.

'Now, the true question is, have we a right to do this? If we have not, all discussions about his comfortable situation and the actual condition of free laborers elsewhere, are quite beside the point. If the Negro has the same right to his liberty and the pursuit of his own happiness that the white man has, and then we commit the greatest wrong and robbery to hold him a slave, an act that which the sentiment of justice must revolt in every heart, and Negro slavery is an institution which that sentiment must sooner or later blot from the face of the earth." – *Richmond Examiner*

'After stating the question, thus, the *Examiner* boldly asserts that the Negro has no such rights – BECAUSE HE IS NOT A MAN. There are three ways to answer this denial, one by ridicule; one by denunciation and one by argument."[3]

But the most important factor here is that Douglass took the time to deconstruct the argument in this speech. He does, without doubt, answer the question of the Negro and his manhood. He lays before his audience the sentiment that should end the dialogue which questions the very character and nature of a human being. Eventually slavery ended, but racism in the nature of the *Richmond Examiner* continued well into the present day, still living on top of a dead system with outmoded ideas, proven wrong time and time again by both sense and sensibility, and, in some cases, through biological and ethnographic studies. But still this debauched philosophy, based on a social system of privilege, refuses to die.

DECONSTRUCTION

The French philosopher Jacques Derrida is called the father of a peculiar tool of literary analysis called deconstruction. Deconstruction began as the way of decoding various signs and symbols in literary text, but has grown to include ways of looking at architecture, law, fashion as well as race. The essence of deconstruction can be posed in two ways. First, "its reason for being is to establish a new center for analyzing the parts or the relationship of parts to meaning, construction and activity." It is about deconstructing and reasserting a new angle of vision on truth.

In Derrida's work, he leads us to the conclusion that Western thought is based on a center, that there is a beginning, and an essence, and normally that beginning in Western culture is in Christianity. In so doing then, Western society marginalizes those who are not part of that center establishment (African American culture is an exception here as the majority are Christian but color and race can be substituted for religion). According to Derrida, working from such a center creates opposites and makes all others either oppositional or marginal to the center. The center of

Western thought – the idea of race as an immutable nature is considered a fact.

We now know that today the deconstruction of race is a dysfunctional political and social factor. The study of the present-day reality of race can be seen in the assigning of individuals to various categories because they possess or acknowledge a heritage which is African. They used to be called many things, mulattoes, quadroons, octoroons, but not generally human beings. Race is so obtuse and that one wonders why anyone recognizes this as important to know. The new context in which mixed-race children and the idea of multiracial has been presented now in the United States, challenges the entire system of race as a real category.

The 2000 U.S. Census allows persons to select more than one of the six categories that were given. Everyone knows this, of course, is not the answer to the question. The fact is that people are refusing to accept labels as handed down by government as a way of defining themselves. Mixed, mixed race, mulatto, biracial, interracial, whatever the category may be, including white, all is in play, and here is the fraying of the issue: how is mixed race different from the entire African-American population in which large numbers of African-Americans, upwards of 80 percent, have at least one ancestor that is not of African descent?

A paper presented by Gina Eric Lee and Professor Chris Nelson called, "The New Vision of Mixed Race: Literary Techniques for Countering Stereotypes," states,

> "Today we hear a lot about Tiger Woods because he defines the rule of hyper descent. He refuses to be classified as black only; he calls himself Cablinasian, a term of his own devising, which represents all four aspects of his racial background. What many people do not realize is that Tiger Woods is not alone. Since the 1967 <u>Loving v. Virginia</u> Supreme Court decision made interracial marriage legal in all states, there has been a mixed-race baby boom."[5]

As members of the first legally recognized generation of mixed-race people increased, many of them are defining themselves as mixed race rather than as monoracial, belonging to one race. As a result, a movement has sprung up to address issues that mixed-race people face. They wish to redefine the one drop rule and lay claim to an individualized version of who they are. Now it could be argued that there is a particular selfishness in this attitude in the sense that at least 80 percent of all African-Americans are of mixed-race descent, but due to historical circumstances, due to the rigidity of racism and segregation laws, and the repeal of marriage laws between whites and blacks, this earlier group of classic African-Americans bound themselves together, both mulatto and African, to create the African-American sensibility in the United States.

This has in fact saved the African-American from being obliterated from the face of the earth.

But whether or not one can undo history is the question. And the answer is no. The point becomes however how does one move forward into the future, and how does one progress beyond the restrictive confines of a definition of race, which was constructed to not only define a lie, but to humiliate and to limit, and denigrate one's personhood. It becomes a question which must be answered. How does one go about answering such a question? The deconstruction then of race is the only way to attempt to lay the groundwork for understanding this complicated set of circumstances.

WE ARE ALL AFRICAN

First, let us look at the biological evidence today, which seems to imply that we are all African. Because out of the "out of Africa" anthropological discoveries, it has almost universally been accepted that mankind originated in Africa, and that all of mankind today is related through biology and genealogy, and there is but one species of mankind. This is the most potent and powerful reordering of the center there could possibly be; however, it is a scientific question and a scientific revelation, meaning there is still more truth and light to come. The center of gravity may move out of Africa to Asia or some other center of discovery, but the trunk and root of the tree today seems to be found only in Africa. The seminal research work on this theory of the African ancestor for all mankind can be found in the work of Spencer Wells, and the work is called, "The Journey of Man", which is excerpted in the following pages. According to Wells,

"Rebecca Cahn, as part of her PhD work in (Allen) Wilson's laboratory began to study the pattern of *mt*DNA variation in humans from around the world. The Berkeley group went to great lengths to collect samples of human placentas (an abundant source of *mt*DNA) from many different populations – Europeans, New Guineans, Native Americans and so on. The goal was to assess the pattern of variation for the entire human species, with the aim of inferring something about human origins. What they found was extraordinary.

'Cann and her colleagues published their initial study of human mitochondrial diversity in 1987. It was the first time that human DNA polymorphism data had been analyzed using parsimony methods to infer a common ancestor and estimate a date. In the abstract to the paper they state the main finding clearly and succinctly: 'All these mitochondrial DNAs stem from one woman who is postulated to have lived about 200,000 years ago, probably in Africa.' The discovery was big news, and this woman became known in the tabloids as Mitochondrial Eve – the mother of us all. In a rather surprising twist, though, she wasn't the only Eve in the garden – only the luckiest.

'The analysis performed by Cahn and her colleagues involved asking how the *mtDNA* sequences were related to each other. In their paper they assumed that if two *mtDNA* sequences shared a sequence variant at a polymorphic site (say, a C at a position where the sequences had either a C or a T), then they shared a common ancestor. By building up a network of the *mt*DNA sequences – 147 in all – they were able to infer the relationships between the individuals who had donated the samples. It was a tedious process, and involved a significant amount of time analyzing the data on a computer. What their results showed were that the greatest divergence between *mt*DNA sequences was actually found among the Africans – showing that they had been diverging for longer. In other words, Africans are the oldest group on the planet – meaning that our species had originated there...[6] Crucially, though, the fact that a single ancestor gave rise to all of the diversity present today does not mean that this was the only person alive at the time – only that the descendant lineages of the other people alive at the same time died out...[6]

...Of course, in the real world, no one transmits a recipe from one generation to the next without modifying it slightly to fit her own tastes. An extra clove of garlic here, a bit more thyme there, and viola! – a bespoke variation on the *matrimoine*. Over time, these variations on a theme will produce their own diversity in the soup bowls – but the recipe extinction continues none the less. If we look at the bespoke village today we see a remarkable diversity of recipes – but they can still be traced back to a single common ancestor in the eighteenth century, thanks to Ock the Knife. This is the secret of Mitochondrial Eve.

...The results from the 1987 study by Cahn and her colleagues were followed up by a more detailed analysis a few years later, and both studies pointed out two important facts: that human mitochondrial diversity had been generated within the past 200,000 years, and that the stone had dropped in Africa. So, in a very short period of time – at least in evolutionary terms – humans had spread out of Africa to populate the rest of the world. There were some technical objections to the statistical analysis in the papers, but more extensive recent studies of mitochondrial DNA have confirmed and extended the conclusions of the original analysis. We all have an African great-great...grandmother who lived approximately 150,000 years ago..."[7]

"Mitochondrial DNA and the Y-chromosome, as we saw before, display deeper lineages within Africa than outside. What does this really mean? If we imagine the genetic relationships among modern mitochondrial diversity as an actual tree – say an oak – then the root and trunk, and the branches that are closest to the ground, are all found in Africa. The branches sprouted first, as the tree was growing, and they are therefore the oldest. This means that the tree started growing in Africa. As we move further up the trunk, the branches start to appear that are found in non-Africans. These formed later. How far up do we have to go before we find the non-Africans? The answer is pretty high. If the tree started growing 150,000 years ago – the age of the root – then the non-African branches are much closer to the top, and do not pre-date 60,000 years. Most of human evolution has been spent in Africa, so it makes sense that there is greater diversity there. Most of the branches on the tree are found only in Africans.

'The beauty of the genetic data is that it gives us a clear, stepwise progression out of Africa into Eurasia and the Americas. The diversity we find around the world is divided into discrete, although related, units, defined by markers – the descendants of ancient mutation events. By mapping these markers onto the map of the world, we can infer details of past migrations. Following the order in which the mutations occurred, and estimating the date and any demographic details (such as population crashes or expansions), we can gain an insight into the details of the journey. And the first piece of evidence comes from one man in particular, who had a rather important, random mutation on his Y-chromosome between 31,000 and 70,000 years ago. He has been named, rather prosaically, M168. More evocatively, he could be seen as the Eurasian Adam – the great...great-grandfather of every non-African man alive today. The journey taken by his sons and grandsons defined the subsequent course of human history... [8]

'As we look more carefully at the arrangement of branches on the mitochondrial tree branches descend from a particular branch of the tree trunk, implying that our M168 Adam was paired with an Eve. Thankfully, this Eurasian Eve lived around 50 – 60,000 years ago, suggesting that she and Eurasian Adam could have met. She is called by the (again) rather mundane name L3, and her daughters accompanied the sons of M168 on their journey to populate the world.

'Based on the distribution of the descendants of M168 and L3 in Africa today, it is likely that they both lived in north-east Africa, in the region of present-day Ethiopia and Sudan. Like all men alive today, M168 shared deeper roots with his African cousins. His lineage is a major branch leading off the human family tree, with his descendant 'terminal branches' found in the DNA of all of today's Eurasians, but he connects them back through M168 to our species' African root. In our tree metaphor, each marker that we study defines the node on the tree – a point where a branch splits into two smaller branches. If we had no marker apart from M168 and L3, our trees would be fairly sparse, comprising a root, (Adam and Eve) and one split on the tree, defined by M168 or L3, on the branch leading out of Africa, and another branch remaining in Africa. Luckily, the tree is packed with dense foliage, defining a pattern of growth that traces the map of our journey." [9]

At this moment, most scientists would agree that mankind originated in Africa around Ethiopia and moved out into the rest of the world. Controversy has arisen over the claim of the one mother Eve-one father Adam theory, but the new DNA called mitochondrial and the Y chromosome has become a new focal point in understanding the relationship of mankind to each other.

It makes sense that we should now spend our time asking about the meaning of life instead of thinking of ourselves as depressed, deprived and defined by an artificial construct for purposes of economic exploitation. Our answer must be to stop the emotional drain that distracts us from greater advancement by taking hold of the dialogue and re-calibrating the race question.

The need to deconstruct race will allow the African-American student to begin the search for a new meaningful life construct. This work could provide reasons to push for an exploration of freedom further and further into the future, so that as William James would have understood, they fill in that open, unfinished world, both physical and social that we inhabit. It will be flushed out in such ways as to accommodate a new sense of identity and dignity. This search for identity is at the heart of the quest for the freedom of the individual. It cannot be an existential exercise.

ENGAGING HBCU STUDENTS AND INSTITUTIONS

The invention of man, it appears, began in Africa. So what does this mean? It only means that there must be a restructuring of how we all approach the issue of human dignity and individuality in the world today. At the heart of this deconstruction is the fact that there are many facets of American life which have been enriched by the circumstances that African-Americans have found themselves in. African-American culture will go nowhere – it is a defining principle in the construction of American Culture. It has been of the most fertile, elastic and engaging aspects of American life, providing America with a base of its classical and popular culture and giving birth to a worldwide popular culture, which is a dynamic force in the world today.

It has produced a leadership that lays claim to asserting and expanding the basic nature of freedom. It will surely rise again with a new platform upon which to stand with race not as a marginalizing force, but as a centralizing idea of the unity of mankind, and will push freedom further for all men and human dignity as a platform in the 21st century. The power of these people as marginalized individuals moving to the center has evoked an entire renaissance of thought and ideas in American society, most importantly redefining the meaning of freedom in western democracy.

BLACKS IN THE GRECO-ROMAN WORLD

The idea now is how do we come to grips with discussing it so that race and prejudice do not dominate our lives, define every situation of life, politically, economically, and socially, even with the knowledge that we have scientifically? It may be that one way we can do this is to discuss prejudice from the point of view of the ancients.

There are possibly two ways to address the issue of defining a new concept of race in this century. The first one would be with students across the Thurgood Marshall College Fund Network, leading dialogues with all state land grand universities in the country. We might look at the Image of Blacks in Western Culture, (based on Howard University's Classics Professor, Frank Snowden's scholarship on Blacks in antiquity) particularly in Europe, and the role of race, color, and culture in the ancient Greco-Roman world, specifically. Such a program could have a two- to four-week curriculum module that could be inserted into introductory and survey courses in the arts, humanities, and social sciences. It would also present programs and activities on campuses to encourage discussion.

Students would be challenged to reconsider the nature of race, and the definition of race, and color prejudice in the ancient Greco-Roman world and how blacks were depicted in Western European art. They would be able to compare and contrast the relative position, attitudes, and public images then and now.

This project would use formal and informal learning environments to help students examine how race, ethnicity, and prejudice were addressed in antiquity. The two-pronged approach centers on innovative exploration into classical literature and art and the creation of a learning-friendly campus ethos. Both approaches use the topic the role of race, color, and culture in the ancient Greco world and the image of blacks in Western European art. The next element is a mechanism to sustain and institutionalize the project. Black students as well as white students will be encouraged to winnow ideas in the literature and art. They will be guided in using those discussions to assist in cultivating and creating a campus ethos that is conducive to academic commitment and a firmament of racial and ethnic diversity. Why is it important to focus on this issue in the Greco-Roman world? The major factor was culture not color or race.

On a broader global scale, it would be important to partner with several organizations to continue to capitalize on several transatlantic dialogues on race and xenophobia that were held in October 2002 sponsored by the European Union Commission, the University of Illinois at Urbana, Howard University, Institute of Government, the University of the District of Columbia, and the Public Affairs Unit at the University of Illinois. These two roundtables took place at the European Parliament in Brussels, Belgium and the United Nations in New York.

The mission of these roundtables was to understand the dynamics surrounding racism and xenophobia in the U.S. and Europe, focusing on majority and minority relations as well as white, black, yellow, brown people and the factors surrounding immigration, social adjustment, and advancement in Western society. The goals were: one, to define the issue of racism and xenophobia as they exist in the beginning of the 21st century; two, to determine and discuss these endeavors, both social, economic, and political, that can be considered best practices so that they can be adapted by governmental and public institutions; three, to build transatlantic networks of practitioners, scholars, and social entrepreneurs to assist in the creation of problem solving programs, meetings, and institutions; four, to develop funding sources to work toward the integration of marginal groups into their respective societies; five, to work for the development of public policy initiatives which government and business and civil society can use as partners to build harmonious, inclusive societies; six, to develop cross-national and cross-cultural networks for youth and adults to broaden horizons of the next generation so that they do not feel isolated and apart from the societies that they live in; seven, to publish recommendations from the conferences and use them to promote public discussion and policy initiatives that will shape and model what Gene Kahn, founding chairman of the European Monitoring Center on Racism and Xenophobia, calls "the reality of diverse peoples living together."

What would take place in these HBCU sponsored roundtables? Experts and scholars would be used to discuss everyday practical events where these issues come into play in lives of individuals, nations, and institutions; clear cut goals will be established by each dialogue and a set of assumption statements developed of what must be accomplished while the dialogues are in process; and, the bulk of the roundtables could be used to discuss best practices for eradicating racism and xenophobic behavior based on our knowledge of the deconstruction of race today.

Civic dialogue uses films, book reviews, and individual testimony to frame the discussion. It has proven to be very effective in illuminating issues and causing people to think deeply about how to solve them based on the two concepts discussed. First, for students and faculty domestically, to discuss culture and race within the confines of an orchestrated, organized, structured dialogue on race and color in the Greco-Roman world, and, secondly, to broaden the dialogue to a transatlantic set of conversations that would bring experts and scholars and practitioners from both sides of the Atlantic to discuss these issues. This would go far in deconstruction and repositioning and redefining race in the 21st century.

Various nations around the world, particularly European and North American, are experiencing great and sometimes all-consuming immigration issues. One of those most contentious of immigration issues is the establishment of an appropriate policy in the United States. It is a question that is important for the intra-group experiences between blacks who have been in America for a long time and are born here and their relationship with immigrants, and then the inter-group conversation, how the America views and deals with African and Latin American immigrants today. If HBCU'S institutions take on this challenge to create these dialogues and to discuss this pervasive issue, it could establish them as major problem-solvers, peacekeepers and resolvers of conflict in the world.

ENCONTRO DAS AGUAS

Encontro das Aguas means in Portuguese the meeting of the waters. This meeting of the waters takes place just outside Manaus, Brazil in the Amazon. It is where two bodies of water, the Yellow River and the Black River, flows side by side for several thousand yards, side by side, never flowing into or collapsing into one another. They remain separate until they eventually empty into each other forming the Great Amazon and become one. While riding down the middle of this truly unusual national occurrence, one can see clearly the tensions of the Old World and the New World, the industrialized and the communal nations, and ultimately, with cooperation, what could happen if we, like the rivers, could finally converge into a mighty life-giving force of humanity.

NOTES

[1]Blummer, Herbert (1958). Race prejudice as a sense of group position. Pacific Sociological Review. (p.4).

[2]Ibid

[3]Frederick Douglas (1854, July 12). The claims of the Negro etymologically considered: An address before the literary societies of Western Reserve College at commencement. Ithaca, NY: The Cornell University Library Digital Collections

[4]Lee, Gina Eric & Nelson, Chris. (1996) The new vision of mixed race: Literary techniques for countering stereotypes. Brown Douglas

[5]Wells, Spencer (2002). The journey of man: The genetic odyssey. Princeton, NJ: Princeton University Press

[6]Ibid (p. 32)

[7]Ibid (pp. 32-33)

[8]Ibid (pp. 70-71)

[9]Ibid (p. 71)

SUMMARY OF
COLLABORATIVE-INNOVATIVE CONCEPTS

The goals of the Acacia initiative are to establish a platform for the discussion of cutting-edge educational issues for HBCUs, and to bring the concept into the educational arena through the media; to support and undergird the development of basic technological structures for faculty and staff; to establish philosophical and theoretical concepts to direct government, business and private funding strategies. In that sense, there are nine outcomes from these papers:

1. The development of a comprehensive youth education policy to replace the fragmented youth development system that now exists from pre-K through graduate school (THE PIPELINE);
2. The creation of the WORLD HOUSE FELLOWS;
3. The establishment of the GATEWAY ACADEMIC PROGRAM (GAP) to fix the leaky pipeline for African-American retention from secondary and post-secondary institutions;

4. The BUILDING OF SUSTAINABLE COMMUNITIES which can undergird economic growth and reweave the fabric of social community;

5. The CONVENING OF RACE DIALOGUES / DIFFICULT DIALOGUES that would bring a new definition of race to American society. This would call for the convening of international round tables and domestic dialogues presented on HBCU campuses and around the world;

6. The development of an education/social infrastructure, a web portal, to undergird the development of the MARSHALL-DU BOIS UNIVERSITY COLLEGES, which would contain the many programs that would connect community and colleges in research and development and growth;

7. The concentrated effort to build a COLLABORATIVE REGIONAL NETWORK OF CBOS AND NGOS to revitalize urban and rural communities, bring about racial reconciliation, and spur economic development, leading to broadening the base of support for HBCU schools;

8. The development of an APPRENTICESHIP STRATEGY;

9. The creation of a COMMUNITY COLLEGE ARTICULATION PLAN that would support both community colleges and the HBCU schools in retention and graduation; and

10. The creation of a FAMILY EDUCATION CONTINUUM that would reinvigorate a family education culture. A system of educational opportunities geared toward families learning together must be developed. Developed around a literacy platform for adult learners and children and delivered via social media, computer based television and radio stations, public access television, and the internet and multi-media educational programs (deliver through the educational great infrastructure) this system could be developed in conjunction with the Land Grant Colleges in each state, and private business entities both for profit and nonprofit.

Appendix A

President Obama's Budget Includes $8 Billion for Community Colleges
2/13/2012

The Obama administration today released an ambitious FY 2013 budget request with many new program proposals to augment already-proposed investments in education and workforce training, job creation, and infrastructure. The budget incorporates and builds upon previous plans such as the American Jobs Act that were designed to enable community colleges to help more Americans secure employment.

The budget includes landmark investments in community colleges, notably an $8 billion "Community College to Career" fund that builds on the Trade Adjustment Assistance Community College and Career Training Grant Program to infuse more resources into job training programs at community colleges. It is designed to train 2 million workers with skills that lead directly to employment. The proposal includes bonus funds for especially effective programs, money for state and local governments to help them attract businesses and jobs to America, and money for entrepreneurship training programs. President Obama introduced this proposal in a speech today at Northern Virginia Community College.

The president also proposes to fund the Pell Grant program at a sufficient level to increase the maximum award to $5,635 in award year 2013–2014, an increase set in motion by the Student Aid and Fiscal Responsibility Act of 2010. The budget also includes previously released proposals for a new $1 billion Race to the Top for higher education institutions and changes to the campus-based aid programs (Federal Work-Study, Supplemental Educational Opportunity Grants, and Perkins Loans) to reward institutions that keep their tuitions down and meet other national goals. It also includes a new $55.5 million "First in the World" fund that would help postsecondary institutions develop and expand innovative and effective strategies for improving college completion. Other key education programs, such as TRIO, GEAR UP, Strengthening Institutions, and programs for minority-serving institutions, would be level-funded. The budget also includes the administration's proposal to reshape the Perkins career and technical education (CTE) programs.

A-1

These investments will require congressional approval, which will be challenging to obtain in the current budget climate and in an election year. Many of the proposals also would require new laws (authorizations) to be enacted in advance of this funding.

APPENDIX B

Aalborg University

Teaching Methods: Aalborg University stands for tradition and innovation. It is rooted in two academic traditions: the classic Danish academic tradition, which historically has developed at the universities, and the professions-oriented tradition, which has been developed at other educational establishments and schools.

Aalborg University combines the two traditions in a broad range of research and educational activities. The classic tradition is represented by a number of disciplines within the Humanities, Natural Sciences and Social Sciences, while the professions-oriented tradition typically is found within the areas of Engineering, Business and parts of the Social Sciences.

Teaching at Aalborg University is research based, which means that the teachers' on-going research is included in teaching with the purpose of bringing the students the most recent scientific knowledge. Furthermore, the University emphasis a continuing development of the teaching methods as well as the teachers' pedagogical qualifications, including the systematic use of information technology in education.

A trademark of Aalborg University is its unique pedagogic model of teaching: the problem-based, project-organized model. With this method, a great part of the teaching and student work throughout the semester revolves around complex real-life problems that the students wonder about and try to find answers to in scientific manners while working together in groups. A recent evaluation from the Organization for Economic Co-operation and Development (OECD) has shown that this form of teaching is close to optimal for the learning process. Project work generally accounts for 50% of the study time at Aalborg University.

Teaching at Aalborg University is also conducted in the forms of lectures, courses, seminars, classroom training, laboratory work and workshops. The use of the different forms of teaching varies depending on the study programme. These forms of studying make up the other 50% of the study time.

Projects and Problem Solving: At Aalborg University, the project work form is at the centre of the teaching methods. A project is a larger assignment within a given framework determined for each semester. The first step in project work is the process of formulating a problem/topic of a theoretical or practical nature. Under tutorial supervision, the students then collect and analyze data and discuss possible solutions to the complex problem.

Through this work process and supported by courses, literature and cooperation with companies and organizations, the students arrive at a deeper understanding of the subject investigated than what they normally would have learned from merely reading and listening. Apart from the strictly professional outcome of this work method, it also brings the students other specific and important qualifications, e.g. good cooperation skills.

At the end of each semester, the project is presented in a written report, which is evaluated orally by the supervisor of the group and an external or internal examiner. The project presented is a comprehensive report of 75 - 150 pages (22500 - 45000 words) depending on the number of contributors.

Group Work: Most students work in groups on the project work. A group is normally between 3 to 5 students. Through the cooperation and division of work that group work allows, the group work provides for the opportunity to investigate more complex and extensive problems than one person normally would be able to do. All project groups have a supervisor to help the group get started, give feedback on the group's work etc.

Group work is not only used in connection with projects, but also in assignment work in e.g. mathematics courses and at the writing of smaller seminar and case assignments.

Courses: A course is a series of lectures on a specific subject area. The form is usually lectures in bigger classes but if it is practical, the students are involved in the teaching by brief presentations at seminars. Some of the courses are related to the broader themes of the semesters and others serve as a direct support to the project work.

Evaluation: Throughout the time of study, the course teachings, the written project work and the written assignments are continuously evaluated. The project reports are usually evaluated by oral group examinations organized in such a way that an individual evaluation of each student takes place as well.

Some courses are directly relevant to the subject of the project work and are evaluated through the project evaluation. Other courses have a broader content and are usually evaluated by individual written or oral examinations.

Aalborg University carries out internal as well as external evaluations. At the internal evaluations, Aalborg University's own academic staff participates as examiners, and at the external evaluations examiners from other universities and the business community participate.

Courses in Pedagogy and Danish Language: In order to get more out of your stay at Aalborg University and in Denmark, it may be a good idea to attend a Danish language class. You can also attend courses in Pedagogy.

Problem based Project Work at Aalborg University: As a student at AAU you will work closely together with your fellow students by way of problem based project work. The Aalborg Model for Problem Based Learning (PBL) enjoys great interest both nationally and internationally, and UNESCO has placed its only Professorial Chair in PBL at AAU.

Problem based project work at Aalborg University: Once you have formed a project group, you need to define a problem together that you want to examine. The problem forms the basis of your project and you are to a great extent responsible for defining this yourselves within a set though often very broad theme frame. See examples of AAU student projects. The project work is completed with an exam. While working on your project, you will also need to do individual exams in your subjects. The project work together with lectures, literature and cooperation with the corporate sector will help you gain a deeper insight into the subject you are examining than if you had been working on your own.

Become well equipped for the modern labour market: The project work at Aalborg University gives you an opportunity to put theoretical knowledge into practice. Often, students at AAU do their project work in cooperation with different enterprises. Just imagine how exciting it is to work with, for instance, a satellite or an advertising campaign in practice. When you work with problems from the 'real world', you reap business experience and perhaps also make good contacts that you can use when applying for a job.

Assistance for project work: For each project, you will be assigned a supervisor, i.e. a professor or another academic member of staff who will guide you in your project work. However, the group has the overall responsibility for defining and writing the project. You will arrange your own supervision meetings with you supervisor. Be aware that, naturally, you do not have an unlimited number of supervision hours available. If in doubt about anything, please do ask your supervisor. The relationship between supervisors/teachers and students at AAU is very informal and usually staff and students are on first-name term with each other.

Literature for the project: Access to articles and literature is vital when you do your project work. In Aalborg, AAU has a large central library (AUB) as well as a number of small subject-specific libraries located across the university. The libraries are well-stocked with regard to electronic editions of recognized journals as well as dissertations, books from the University's own press, common literature etc. AUB is very popular both as a library and a place of work particularly for international students.

Group Work at Aalborg University: At Aalborg University, students usually do their problem based project work in groups. Typically, you will be part of a group consisting of 4-5 students. Each semester, the group completes a large assignment called a project. You form the groups yourselves depending on your academic interests.

The advantages of group work at AAU: The group work ensures a great variety of approaches and perspectives, which results in a sound and thoroughly prepared project. Together, you are able to discuss the details thoroughly. At the same time, you are able to solve larger and more complex problems than if you were studying on an individual basis. Each of you has the opportunity to shape the project because group work requires that everyone contributes. If you have any academic questions you may also discuss these with your friends in the group.

You learn how to cooperat: During group work you will quickly realise that you might have different opinions about how to solve a problem. Group work means that you have to compromise and you will learn a lot about how to cooperate. Group work is very popular on the modern labour market so both you and your future workplace will benefit from the skills in cooperation you have acquired at AAU.

Make new friends: When you work in a group you spend quite some time together and you will quickly get to know your fellow students. You plan your own work hours, which makes it possible to do other things apart from project work. Group work gives you a chance to meet new friends with whom you can go to the cinema or a café in your spare time. If you prefer working on your own, this is also possible. Project work in groups throughout your entire education is not a requirement at AAU.

Group rooms at Aalborg University: A large part of Aalborg University consists of group rooms where you can meet up and discuss your project. However, you must be prepared to share the room with other groups as the number of group rooms at AAU is not unlimited. Usually, this does not cause any problems and in some cases it might actually help inspire your project work. It is up to you how often you want to use the group room – presupposing, of course, that it is vacant. You may also choose to hold work meetings at home or at <u>Aalborg University Library, AUB</u>, which is very popular amongst international students.

Teaching methods at Aalborg University: At Aalborg University, a large part of your knowledge is acquired through project work with your group, but also through more traditional teaching methods. The relationship between teachers and students is dialogue-based and very informal, so do ask if in doubt about anything.

Teaching methods at Aalborg University: At Aalborg University you will attend several courses, also known as lectures. You are responsible for your own learning and so, attending the lectures is a good idea. Depending on what you study, the teaching form may span from seminars to laboratory work and typically you will be taught by a lecturer. During a semester, you will have 2 to 6 series of lectures each consisting of up to 15 lectures. A distinction is made between two types of lectures : Project unit courses and study unit courses.

Inspiration for the project: During project unit courses, you and your group can find inspiration for your project if you are finding it difficult to decide on a topic and a problem. The series of lectures falls within the overall theme of the individual semester and gives you an insight into a specific subject. The lecturer will go over e.g. methods and theories that you can use in the project.

General lectures at AAU: The study unit courses give you a more general basic knowledge within your subject area and provide breadth in your education. Sometimes the lecturer might encourage you and your fellow students to actively participate in the teaching, for instance, by doing a presentation. This is a very educational experience and therefore an opportunity you should embrace.

Dedicated lecturers: At Aalborg University you will be presented with the most recent scientific knowledge within the different research areas and you are taught by dedicated lecturers. Teaching at AAU is research-based as your lecturers conduct research in the subject area that they teach. Therefore, the educational material often comprises articles from current journals. If you have any academic questions, just ask your lecturer.

External knowledge: During your studies, you will get a chance to hear more about how the theories and methods you are being taught can be used in practice.

B-6

Some teachers at AAU invite people from e.g. the corporate sector to do guest lectures. On other occasions, the University will hold conferences etc. where you can hear a 'guru' within your subject area. These opportunities should never be missed.

Continuing Education: With the changes in society towards a situation in which knowledge is a central competitive parameter, the need for continuing education is increasing.

Aalborg University currently strengthens Continuing Education in order to provide academics with enhanced possibilities to develop their competences by participating in the broad selection of the University's master's programmes, part-time master's programmes, single subjects, tailor made courses, long distance teaching, the vacant seat scheme etc.

In the next few years, Aalborg University will continue to offer relevant continuing education, including programmes which will contribute to strengthening cooperation with small and medium sized companies.

APPENDIX C

UNIVERSITY OF THE DISTRICT OF COLUMBIA LORTON PRISON

The District of Columbia Correctional Facility located at Lorton, hereafter referred to simply as Lorton, is composed of three (3) facilities, minimum, medium and maximum security. The UDC college program at Lorton is administered jointly through the Division of Continuing Education at UDC in conjunction with the four (4) departments which offer a degree program at Lorton: Urban Studies (for which department the author teaches at Lorton), Library/Media Technology, Health, and Accounting and by the D.C. Department of Corrections through its Office of Program Coordination. The UDC program is offered to eligible residents in medium security at Lorton. Some from the minimum security facility about two (2) miles away from the medium security facility are bussed in. Those in maximum security are not eligible to take the program.

The present research was designed to evaluate the UDC program at Lorton and to compare men who are in the program with those who are not. Later, we will compare ex-offenders from Lorton who have had a UDC education with ex-offenders from Lorton who did not have a UDC education, so as to compare the two (2) groups as to the rates of employment, rehabilitation and recidivism. Then, we will look at a sample of District men with and without a college education who have never been incarcerated to examine the role of a UDC education in their lives. In all cases, the men we speak of are Black males from the inner highest T C and I scores of the Lorton sample. We were aware of very high moral among the research team; however, we do not know the exact reason for this high morale, and for the Team scoring highest of the three (3) groups of the sample, and higher than Peace Corp Volunteers on the I Score. What did we do right? Why did they put so much effort into the work they did and carry out interviews against such adverse conditions as refusals to answer questions or getting bloody noses if the respondent objected to being asked questions at all. The Research Team knew ahead of time that it would be difficult to get responses in this "hostile environment," as some of them phrased it, where questions were definitely discouraged or responded to threateningly.

C-1

Was it the team work? Was it the feeling of doing something important? Was it the attention they were getting from the staff at Lorton and the knowledge that they were the first known residents to be trained in and to carry out a research project?

We will carry out an intensive follow-up of the 25 men who were involved in the Research Team over two (2) semesters, and find out what they felt about this experience.

We might also administer the POI test to them again, a year after this experience, to see if the good feelings they had at the time have been lasting, or were part of the then, present feelings.

However, the hypothesis that the UDC sample would score higher on the POI measure than the non-UDC sample, was supported by the findings. An unexpected and gratifying finding was that the men who worked with the author or the Research Team, helping to design the research, contacting respondents, carrying out interviews and coding the data, scored as highly as non-incarcerated high scoring Peace Corp Volunteers.

CONTRIBUTIONS

This study has made the following contributions to an evaluation of the impact of higher education of an adult population and one incarcerated in a correctional institution.

This is the first empirically known research testing differences and using a control group, between residents of a correctional institution, Lorton D.C. Correctional Facility, enrolled or not enrolled in the UDC College Program at Lorton.

This work has formed the background for a new hypothesis, to be tested in the next phase of the research, to the effect that among those leaving Lorton in the next year, those with college education will have significantly lower rates of recidivism, and a better work history than those who were not enrolled in the UDC College Program at Lorton.

This research has enabled us to identify at least one (1) set of residents in a correctional facility with the potential for a high rate of success since we have found that those in the UDC program at Lorton differ from the non-UDC residents of the sample in the following ways:

The UDC group comes from a higher income, family background with more education and less family cultural and economic deprivation;

The UDC enrolled student is better prepared work-wise for release with more skills and more white-collar skills than the non-UDC resident

The UDC resident tends to be a one-time offender with more chances of rehabilitation than the career-criminal non-UDC resident;

The peer group of the UDC resident is composed of fewer friends and relatives with a history of deviant behavior;

The policy implications are obvious. The program was closed by the DC government in the late 1990's.

UNIVERSITY OF THE DISTRICT OF COLUMBIA
LORTON PRISON COLLEGE PROGRAM, DECEMBER 1996

HISTORY OF THE LORTON PRISON COLLEGE PROGRAM

The University of the District of Columbia's Lorton Project resulted from a joint effort of the University and the District of Columbia Department of Corrections. James Freeman, John H. Johnson and William Jefferson of the Department of Corrections, and Andress Taylor of the University of the District of Columbia began talking about a prison college program in 1968 when they realized that existing programs at Lorton were not meeting the needs of highly motivated inmates. Additionally, a change in the mental attitudes of the men was required to reduce the odds of their returning to prison once released.

The Lorton Project, as it was known in the beginning, became a reality in March 1969. Forty-seven inmates at Central Facility, Lorton, Virginia (which included Youth Centers I and II), were enrolled in the Lorton Project of Federal City College, which later became part of the University of the District of Columbia. The project, utilizing the concepts of self-awareness, education, and community involvement, has been successful. Its goals eventually were expanded to that of a comprehensive degree-oriented program for inmates and former inmates of the Department of Corrections. During the 10 years of the program's existence, approximately 70 inmates have been awarded A.A. and B.A. degrees prior to leaving Lorton. Many others have received degrees after their release.

Recidivism among graduates of the Lorton Prison College Program is very limited. To a great extent, it appears, higher education provides program participants with the tools to fashion a different lifestyle and break the cycle of crime, arrest and incarceration.

Lorton Library Program

The Lorton Library was established in 1979 out of a need to enhance the Federal City College educational program. This program was initiated under the leadership of Professor Janette Hoston Harris who taught African American History and served as President of the District of Columbia chapter of the National Hook-up of Black Women (D C Hook-Up). The Chapter solicited books from the Washington community and built the first library at Lorton with more than 400 books and over one hundred magazines. The program continued for four years with bi-monthly book contributions to the program.

Below is the Institutional Phase statistical report of the UDC Lorton program for the period of 1969-1996

- **3,180** or more residents at Lorton have participated to some degree in the Lorton Prison College Program.
- Students are currently enrolled, either full-time or part-tiome, in the Lorton Prison College Program.
- **25%** of the UDC students presently at Lorton are high school graduates: 4% of these have attended college previously.
- 110 Students are currently enrolled in the pre-college program.
- **75%** of the UDC students presently at Lorton successfully completed GED requirements and were admitted to the Program on that basis.
- **225** UDC students at Lorton have made the Dean's List: 65 have graduated with honors.
- **289** students who have participated in the institutional phase of the program have graduated from the University with the Associate degree.
- 93 students who have participated in this Program have graduated from the University or its predecessor institution (Federal City College) with the baccalaureate degree.
- **321** degrees have been awarded at the summer commencement by students who completed all degree work at Lorton.
- 19 UDC Summer commencement ceremonies have been held at the Lorton Facility.
- 28 is the average age of UDC students at Lorton.

- 186 UDC students at Lorton have earned busing privileges and have taken classes on the Main campus while still incarcerated (from September 1970 to 1985).
- 152 different college-level courses have been taught at four Lorton facilities through this Program.
- **50%** of the current Lorton Prison College Program faculty hold the doctoral degree and 50% hold the master's as the highest degree earned.
- 27 years represents the period of continuous operation of this Program.
- **15%** of the students in the Program on an average for any given semester
- **6-10%** represents the rate of recidivism for graduates of the Lorton Prison College Program as compared to a national average of over 40% for inmates returned to urban communities for similar periods of time.

Program Goals

- To provide some of the inmates with access to courses at the institutional level while others, such as inmates from Federal institutions will have access to on-campus classes at the University.
- To provide and administer college level education and services for that segment of the prison population that is motivated and capable and for whom most prison programs are not intellectually challenging.
- To develop a pool of inmates who can serve as constructive role models within the prison system and later in the inner city.

Program Objectives

- To provide core courses that will lead to matriculation toward college degrees
  - To schedule and implement core courses in Legal Assistance Technology.
  - To schedule and implement core courses in Computer Science Technology

D-3

- To schedule and implement core courses in Accounting Technology
- To schedule and implement core courses in Media Technology
- To schedule and implement core courses in Urban Studies
- To provide, where possible, the scheduling of additional programs and general elective courses with consideration given to input from the D.C. Department of Corrections.

- To increase the enrollment of individuals serving longer terms who provide a nucleus for the design of long range-academic planning.
- To provide opportunity for development of leadership skills and styles through the Lorton Student Government Association.

Extracurricular Activities

In addition to the academic component of the Lorton Prison College Program, the inmates participated in other activities, such as the Cultural Arts Forums, the Student Government, and the Student Newsletter.

Cultural Arts Forum

Under this program, established in Fall Semester 1970 as the Distinguished Lecture Series, scholars, community leaders, and professionals impart ideas and concepts and provide information to residents that would otherwise be inaccessible to them.

Although the forum is aimed at the college program students, the events were open to all inmates at the Correctional Complex.

Student Government

A branch of the University of the District of Columbia's Student Government Association (the voice of the student body) was organized at Lorton by students in the college program. This branch of the SGA represents students enrolled at the institution and those in the busing and on-campus phases of the program. A primary function of Lorton's student government is to provide residents with

D-4

experience in budgeting, parliamentary procedures, program planning, leadership, and general governing problems and responsibilities. The Lorton student government is comprised of seven departments: Legal Affairs, Planning and Research, Student Activities, Pre-College Program, Student Affairs, Community Relations, and the Student Newsletter.

Student Newsletter

The student newsletter, the People's Press, was initiated in February 1975 by members of the Lorton Prison College Program and was staffed solely by Lorton Prison College Program students. It proved to be an outlet for creative expression and a source of information about the daily events of the Lorton Correctional Facility.

Based on a report by Dr. Ernesta Pendleton Williams, UDC Staff; Janice Borlandoe, Acting VP for Student Affairs; Bobby Austin, Vice President for University Relations and Executive Secretary to the Board of Trustees; Denise Kinlaw, UDC Staff.

APPENDIX E

HISTORICAL OVERVIEW THIRTY YEARS OF CONSOLIDATION

BACKGROUND

The University of the District of Columbia was conceived, developed, and created in a vortex of extremely complex, political, economic, social and educational cross-currents. The history of our creation is rich and deserves to be told as a classic tale of ecstasy and agony. It is the story of an earnest desire to provide high quality low cost education to the residents of the District of Columbia, and it is the story of the complicated process that can entangle any higher education endeavor.

But more, the process we have been through and continue to go through is the stuff with which all reality-makers must contend with and sort out as they try to implement the visionaries dream. It has not been easy. Our story is the model for those who wish to see firsthand and up close just what it feels like to reorder a universe of independent heavenly bodies, each supreme within its own orbit. It is not a job for mere mortals. Yet we admit openly that we are mortals. And we have had some spectacular successes and in turn, some dismal failures. Yet we look forward to our thirteenth birthday conscious of our predecessor institutions; a history and legacy that stretches back over a century. We are confident in the face of praise, condemnation, acclaim and intrigue; we are unwavering. The University of the District of Columbia will continue to develop and fulfill its dream and its mission.

In this, the Capital of the United States and the free World, a city itself still in the shadows of political dependence, a breathtaking idea was born; the establishment of an Urban Land Grant University. The idea itself captures the essence of the founding of this republic and American public higher education. By creating UDC as an 1862 Land Grant Institution, the extension of full rights and responsibilities of mass public education at its finest was given. This prized land grant status is a promise of real hope for the citizens of the District, but at present we have not fully capitalized on it.

E-1

Fortunately for the development of the comprehensive State University, and for all of American higher education, the Morrill Land-Grant College Act, signed into law by President Abraham Lincoln on July 2, 1862, was one of the most beautifully vague pieces of legislation in the history of education, and therein lies much of its greatness...

This broad charter initiated a revolution in higher education and fortunately—in part because it was obviously open to a wide range of interpretation—an affirmative revolution. It did not seek to eliminate or denigrate existing disciplines, or areas of professional emphasis, but to open up higher education to new disciplines and new professions.

Jonathan Baldwin Turner had defined the "industrial classes" of the time as 95 percent of the people, charging that existing colleges served only five percent of the population -- the "literary" and "leisure" classes. He had no objection to serving the five percent in his new universities, if the needs of the 95 percent were met. The Land-Grant Act of 1862 may be regarded as a broad charter, similar to the U.S. Constitution, emphasizing certain major principles, rather than providing a detailed prescription... This is the tradition into which UDC was born and it continues its birthright and builds upon its principles.

THE INITIAL STUDY

The April of 1971, the District government contracted with A.D. Little, Inc., to undertake an analysis of public higher education in D.C. The firm prepared the report and delivered it to the D.C. Government in December 1972.

The Arthur D. Little study recommended a system of four, possibly three, differentiating institutions operating under a governing board. The report recommends that at the system level, the Chancellor would administer senior staff units to assist the Board and Chancellor in overall system planning and management. The four differentiating institutions recommended that the components of the system include:

- A four-year comprehensive college
- An institute of technology
- A University center

E-2

- A comprehensive multi-campus community college.

Alternately, three institutions could be established:

- A comprehensive four-year college
- A University center
- A multi-campus community college

HEARINGS ON H.R. 15643

By 1973 the U.S. Congress, through the House District Committee, chaired by Congressman Diggs, held hearings on H.R. 15643. The hearings saw scores of D.C. educators, politicians, and citizens testify before it. Some were for, and of course, some were against.

But because our focus is on structure, we would like to call to your attention the testimony of Dr. Marjorie Parker, then a D.C. Councilmember, and former University of the District of Columbia Board of Trustees Chairman. Dr. Parker stated:

"The Council believes that a University system would provide a legal mechanism within which greater coordination and unification of public higher education could be accomplished. Additionally, this legislation could be expected to bring further cohesiveness of purpose and of goals with maximum and equitable utilization of funds and resources. A University system as conceived in this bill, with distinct colleges and schools, including graduate programs and post graduate programs, will provide a wide range of opportunity for all residents of the District of Columbia. Students with varying abilities, and I might say interests, but who for financial reasons cannot take advantage of the programs offered by the many fine Universities in the area will have access to a multiplicity of opportunities with the envisioned public University.

In answer to questions from the Committee with respect to the A.D. Little study and the cost to D.C. citizens, if all the institutions remained distinct but within a system which would continue to expand and grow, where would the savings be, and especially if H.R. 15643 was based on such a premise. Ms. Ruby

Martin, then the Assistant Council to the Committee, reiterated from Dr. Parker's statement that the bill before them sought to "reorganize the existing three local public institutions of public higher education" new academic programs and new offerings would be contained with this new consolidated structure.

The key argument for organizing public higher education in the District was the need for broader academic program offerings and to curtail escalating cost of maintaining three separate institutions. Thus, fiscal prudence and educational opportunity were to go hand-in-hand. It is important to note this exchange of ideas regarding interest, as we believe it sets the tone for the development of a consolidated University as opposed to a system of independent institutions.

D.C. LAW 1-36

In October of 1974, Public Law 93-471 (H.R. 15643), was enacted. Thus the framework and vision for the University had been established. Now what did the new law say and do. P.L. 93-471 became D.C. Law 1-36 in November 1975. "By approving the congressional intent to establish the University of the District of Columbia, the law provided the framework for how the consolidation was to occur.

The law, D.C. Law 1-36 Section 205, stipulated that the "trustees shall by September 1, 1976, consolidate the existing public institutions of postsecondary education in the District of Columbia under a single management system to be called the University of the District of Columbia, with several programs, schools, colleges, institutes, campuses and other components that offer a comprehensive program of public postsecondary education . The institutions of public postsecondary education in the District of Columbia existing immediately prior to such consolidation shall be deemed abolished on the effective date of the consolidation. Thereafter, any reference in any law, rule, regulation, or other document of the United States or the District of Columbia to such institutions shall be deemed to be a reference to the University of the District of Columbia."

The Charter Board was seated in May of 1976. Ronald H. Brown was elected as the Board's first Chairman. This Board faced a monumental task but they were able to succeed by using D.C. Law 1-36, the enabling legislation, literally as a bible for direction. After organizing themselves and providing for a structure of committee operations as contained in the Board's By-laws, which is still in use today, they set about the task of consolidation.

MISSION STATEMENT

The Educational Policy Committee (EPC) was charged with two major tasks by the Chairman of the Board. This first task was to develop a proposed structure for the new University by December 31, 1976. The second was organization of the curricula so that they would be compatible with the new structure. In order that this consolidation process might move in a coordinated fashion, EPC set about to develop a mission statement which would guide it in its development of a cohesive and sound theoretical framework for our consolidated University. The mission statement is as follows:

Early in our nation's history, access to higher education was limited primarily to those pursuing careers in the ministry, medicine, and law. Later, with the advent of the land-grant college system, higher education expanded its mission to meet the demands of an industrial and agrarian society. This involved not only the training of young men and women for a variety of careers, but also the development of scholars and researchers in the humanities and the natural and social sciences. During the past hundred years our colleges and universities have played a major role in providing the nation with scientific technology, an educated leadership and an ever increasing level of literacy among the mass of citizens.

Now, as our nation enters its third century, higher education must reaffirm its commitment to improving the quality of life by providing instruction, advanced technology, career preparation, and education in the liberal arts toward the maximum development of the individual and the community.

Among the land-grant institutions of America, the University of the District of Columbia has a unique opportunity to direct the land-grant traditions of teaching, research, and extension to urban problems. Aware of the urgent need for strengthening intra-cultural harmony, the University is committed to fostering an appreciation of the variety of cultural styles which characterize our city and the American people. The University of the District of Columbia will strive for excellence in meeting higher education needs and aspirations of the people of the nation's capital at the lowest possible cost to the student.

To accomplish its goals, the University shall:

- Maintain an admissions policy which reflects the needs, aspirations, and character of the residents of the District of Columbia;
- Create a University environment which fosters academic and cultural development wherein liberal studies embody an appreciation for the professional, vocational; and technical and undergirded by the liberal and humane uses of technology;
- Provide counseling and other services to assist students in discovering and developing their potential;
- Offer a comprehensive program of studies which responds to the widest range of needs and aspirations of residents of the community recognizing that learning is a life-long process;
- Engage in research and public service programs serving the people of the community and the District and Federal governments;
- Offer vocational and career development which meets the requirements of the community and increases the career options of District residents;
- Prepare practitioners for positions of leadership in the various professions;
- Offer such credit and non-credit seminars, forums, courses, and institutes as will enrich the lives of District residents including activities designed to upgrade skills, introduce cultural and recreational activities, and assist in leadership training;
- Provide for faculty, student, and community participation in developing and evaluating the University's programs and services;
- Maintain cooperative relationships with:
  - ➢ The D.C. public school system for mutual efforts in improving public education at all levels;
  - ➢ Public and private postsecondary institutions in the community;
  - ➢ Industry, business, and government agencies for internship opportunities;

E-6

> The many cultural, educational, and international resources which abound in Washington;

> The media;

> Civil and professional organizations

This statement was drafted and presented to college Presidents for distribution to members of the University community for their input. After an intensive effort on the part of faculty, the draft mission statement was adopted on September 14, 1976, with an added suggestion of Dr. Sarah Pereira to include among our ideals something on "world-wide service/attainment."

PROPOSED STRUCTURE

From there, EPC began to carry out the first phase of its charge from the Board which was to develop the structure from which UDC would operate. At the July 27, 1976 meeting of EPC, the Presidents of the various campuses were asked to appoint three representatives from each institution. These persons were to set up a task force which would work in collaboration with Board members on the consolidated structure.

Dr. Fields of WTI (Washington Technical Institute) was appointed the convener. This task force began its role very quickly. They spent several months in deliberation and thought. Throughout the summer months EPC and the Task Force worked individually to develop a sound structure. September 14, 1976, a position paper emphasized the need to preserve a portion of the identity of the existing schools but not in their entirety.

On September 14, 1976, EPC hired Dr. I. Tribble to act as an expert educational consultant for structure and curriculum. Dr. Tribble was given a written plan of activities and began his work. He subsequently held meetings with Dr. Wendell Russell, Dr. Ron Williams, Dr. William Crump, Dr. Julius Mack, Dr. Ken Tollett, Mr. Ron Brown, Dr. Joan Williams, Dr. Thomas, and Dr. Estelle Taylor. These meetings were held by the consult so that he might more effectively bring to the committee the opinions and thoughts of the University community. He would then be able to demonstrate this thought through his development of the structure that would be proposed to EPC. This process lasted from September 27,

1976 to October 25, 1976. Dr. Tribble made his presentation, a preliminary report for review and discussion, on October 25, 1976. A work session was held by the Board on this matter which also involved the Task Force.

After hearing the Tribble report, the task force made its report on November 1, 1976. It was made by Dr. William Crump, and this report was followed by a minority report given by Dr. Fields of the Van Ness Campus. EPC reviewed all three reports and instructed the consultant to attempt to reconcile those areas where differences appeared so that we might have a broadly acceptable structure. Dr. Tribble revised his report and submitted a revised effort which took into account the majority/minority reports. EPC, after much discussion, received his report and after due consideration proposed to the Board, On December 7, 1976, through resolution number UDC76-25, that this version be received by the Board and reviewed by the University and the general community. The resolution was sent to the D.C. Register and published on December 26, 1976.

CALENDAR

A Task Force to coordinate the study of a calendar for UDC was appointed on September 16, 1976. Mr. Alton Wilson was designated as Chairman. This task force was created to study calendar plans and to make recommendations to EPC on this matter. Again, the task force was composed of personnel from our three institutions. Mr. Wilson completed his work prior to the December 7 Board meeting at which time the Chairperson of EPC introduced resolution UDC 76-24, which would fix the UDC calendar on a early semester plan. This was adopted by the Board.

Consequently, the first phase of work which EPC had been charged to carry out by December 21, 1976, had been met. A structure for UDC had been proposed and a calendar system had been set. EPC could now move into the second phase of its work, curriculum. The Chairperson of the Committee issued a memorandum to the Presidents to pick those persons they felt could be of service in the development of a consolidated curriculum. This task force relied heavily on the academic deans of UDC for leadership and guidance.

E-8

30 YEARS OF CONSOLIDATION 30 YEARS OF INNOVATION
UNIVERSITY COLLEGE AS THE OPEN GATE TO THE UNIVERSITY

The concept of a University college was developed in consonance with what was interpreted as the legislative intent as so stated in D.C. LAW No. 1-36. Additionally it is the clear and specific intent of the Council of the District of Columbia that the University provide a range of programs, studies and degrees to reach the widest possible number of citizens and residents of the District of Columbia including career and technological education, liberal arts, sciences, teacher education; and associate general, postgraduate and professional degrees and studies.... The function of the board is to build a University to serve the residents of the District of Columbia consisting of but not limited to, strong programs of liberal arts studies and vocational-technical education in accordance with the provisions of this Act.

There appeared to be three crucial policy indicators for Board implementation in the above concept: (1) a range of programs, studies and degrees; (2) to reach the widest possible number of citizens and residents; and (3) strong programs of liberal arts studies and vocational-technical education. A strict interpretation of the law would see it as being much more prescriptive in nature than permissive.

Thus, to comply with the intent of the law it would be necessary for the Board to satisfy the explicit as well as the implicit framework provided.

Therefore, the conception of the University of the District of Columbia begins with a range of academic objectives that move from the certificate and diploma levels to the doctoral and professional levels.

The question of open admission needs further explanation. The legislation as mentioned earlier has provided some broad direction for admission policy. The experience of the three institutions being merged to form the foundation of the University also adds to this matrix. The Board was charged with providing more specific direction with regard to admissions policy. In addition, The University College was seen as the place where students would be introduced to the University. This introduction should be of the highest quality, informative, with

F-1

standards and expectations of UDC and the general environment very supportive and professional.

Open admissions for UDC was interpreted to mean that for those who wish to enter and have successfully completed high school or have obtained a GED diploma and who are judged by faculty and admissions staff as capable of making reasonable progress after enrollment, should be admitted. It was anticipated that the above admissions criteria would produce a diverse group of students in every respect. For reasons it would be necessary for the University College to have programs ranging from honors through pre-collegiate which would require extensive supportive service efforts.

Open admission in the past and currently can mean a revolving door for many students. It was thought that this was an area in which UDC could almost immediately distinguish itself in the field of post-secondary education by reversing this negative trend. UDC was not alone in finding itself faced with the failure of many secondary schools. However, the Board viewed the task of making up high school deficiencies as a short term goal for the University. The long range goal would be to shift this burden back to the secondary schools and then reallocate those resources to the traditional business of the University.

The idea that the "best teachers" should be sought for service in the University College was not a completely novel idea. There has been much debate over the years about rewarding good just as good research and service is rewarded within the University setting. Also, too often the "best teachers" seem to be reserved for those students who probably need them less. Here it was argued that the University College needed the "best teachers" available who are tried and tested in the urban environment and who desire to teach a diverse group of students with acknowledgement of educational deficiencies.

As UDC viewed the traditional tripartite mission of the University, clearly undergraduate teaching was the highest priority initially.

Community service would represent the second highest priority and selected research and graduate teaching its third priority.

The University College was a highly innovative educational concept in 1976. UDC developed one of the first such units in the Nation. The University College closed in 1996.

Assumptions:

1. University College is a major priority for the University

2. The allocation of resources will reflect the importance of this priority to the University.

University College

Core Courses

For all students who enter the University at the lower division

Improvement Clinic

Activities, minicourses, transition courses, independent studies designed to upgrade skills of lower division students

Counseling Clinic

Specially geared for the kinds of problems plaguing lower division educationally disadvantaged students

Test & Measurements

Diagnostic services for lower division students designed to pinpoint learning difficulties and abilities

Relation Research

On-going research to ascertain methods and conditions required to teach the educationally disadvantage

APPENDIX G

OUR ACHIEVEMENT-GAP MANIA, Frederick M. Hess

A decade ago, the No Child Left Behind Act ushered in an era of federally driven educational accountability focused on narrowing the chasms between the test scores and graduation rates of students of different incomes and races. The result was a whole new way of speaking and thinking about the issue: "Achievement gaps" became reformers' catch phrase, and closing those gaps became *the* goal of American education policy.

Today, the notion of "closing achievement gaps" has become synonymous with education reform. The Education Trust, perhaps the nation's most influential K-12 advocacy group, explains: "Our goal is to close the gaps in opportunity and achievement." The National Education Foundation has launched its own "Closing the Achievement Gaps Initiative." The California Achievement Gap Educational Foundation was launched in 2008 to "eliminate the systemic achievement gap in California K-12 public education." Elite charter-school operator Uncommon Schools says its mission is running "outstanding urban charter public schools that close the achievement gap and prepare low-income students to graduate from college." *Education Week*, the newspaper of record for American education, ran 63 stories mentioning "achievement gaps" in the first six months of this year.

The No Child Left Behind Act's signal contribution has been this sustained fixation on achievement gaps — a fixation that has been almost universally hailed as an unmitigated good. Near the end of his presidency, George W. Bush bragged that NCLB "focused the country's attention on the fact that we had an achievement gap that — you know, white kids were reading better in the 4th grade than Latinos or African-American kids. And that's unacceptable for America." Margaret Spellings, Bush's secretary of education, said last year, "The raging fire in American education is the achievement gap between poor and minority students and their peers."

Indeed, at the elite level, there is bipartisan consensus on this question. President Obama has echoed Bush, terming education the "civil-rights issue of our time" and explaining that his agenda is intended to address "the pervasive achievement gap between today's black and white students." Obama's secretary of education, Arne Duncan, repeated the familiar formulation last year at the National Press Club, declaring: "The achievement gap is unacceptable. Education is the civil-rights issue of our generation."

Such sentiments are admirable, and helping the lowest-achieving students do better is of course a worthy and important aim. But the effort to close gaps has hardly been an unmitigated blessing. In their glib self-confidence, the champions of that effort have refused to confront its costs and unintended consequences, and have been far too quick to silence skeptics by branding them blind defenders of the status quo (if not calling them outright racists).

The truth is that achievement-gap mania has led to education policy that has shortchanged many children. It has narrowed the scope of schooling. It has hollowed out public support for school reform. It has stifled educational innovation. It has distorted the way we approach educational choice, accountability, and reform.

And its animating principles — including its moral philosophy — are, at best, highly questionable. Indeed, the relentless focus on gap-closing has transformed school reform into little more than a less objectionable rehash of the failed Great Society playbook.

CHANGING EDUCATION'S MISSION

The 21st-century education debate bears witness to the political genius of Marian Wright Edelman, founder of the Children's Defense Fund, who had the foresight to repackage the social-welfare agenda of the Great Society by putting children front and center. While this tactic yielded some real benefits, highlighting the needs of young people who were too long marginalized or ignored, it has also distorted our understanding of schools and their mission.

Today, debates about the purpose and provision of education — on the left and the right alike — are reduced to platitude-laden charges that it is up to schools to do what the social reformers of the 1960s could not accomplish through entitlements, social-welfare programs, or other Great Society initiatives. Along the way, reformers have casually abandoned more ambitious visions of democratic education, as well as the credo that every child deserves an opportunity to fulfill his potential. It is crucial to recognize that "reformers," not educators, have driven this shift: In a 2008 survey, for instance, education pollsters Steve Farkas and Anne Duffett asked, "For the public schools to help the U.S. live up to its ideals of justice and equality, do you think it's more important that they focus equally on all students regardless of their backgrounds or achievement levels . . . or disadvantaged students who are struggling academically?" Eighty-six percent of teachers said all students and just 11% said disadvantaged students. Yet education reformers are doing their very best to counter this healthy democratic impulse — and they have largely succeeded.

Today, school reformers, state and local education officials, exemplary charter-school operators, and managers of philanthropic foundations make it very clear that they are primarily in the business of educating poor black and Hispanic children. Indeed, anyone who has spent much time in the company of school reformers in the past decade has seen this practice turn almost comical, as when charter-school operators try to one-up one another over who can claim the most disadvantaged student population.

All of this has eroded traditional notions of what constitutes a complete education. Because of the way "achievement gaps" are measured — using scores on standardized reading and math tests — any effort to "close the achievement gap" must necessarily focus on instruction in reading and math. Hence many schools, particularly those at risk of getting failing grades under NCLB, have fixated on reading and math exclusively; other subjects — art and music, foreign language, history, even science — have been set aside to make more time and resources available for remedial instruction. The *New York Times* has reported that, in Sacramento, California, poorly performing students are permitted to enroll only in math, reading, and gym, in a mad dash to help close the achievement gap. The *Wall Street Journal* has reported that, facing budget pressures and a relentless press to drive up reading and math scores among the least proficient students, school districts nationwide are axing foreign-language instruction. Indeed, according to the Center for Applied Linguistics, between 1997 and 2008, the share of U.S. elementary schools offering foreign-language classes fell by roughly one-fifth.

These developments have compromised schools' ability to cultivate students' aptitudes and talents. For instance, Therese Sullivan Caccavale — former president of the National Network for Early Language Learning — has noted that research shows that "[c]hildren who learn a foreign language beginning in early childhood demonstrate certain cognitive advantages over children who do not . . . [and] children who study a foreign language, even when this second language study takes time away from the study of mathematics, outperform (on standardized tests of mathematics) students who do not study a foreign language and have more mathematical instruction during the school day."

Lost too has been an appreciation of schools' broader mission. For American founders like Benjamin Rush and Thomas Jefferson, the primary function of schooling was to produce democratic citizens. In Rush's telling phrase, schools needed to mold "republican machines." Yet in a 2010 survey, 70% of high-school social-studies teachers reported that civics has been marginalized by the focus on reading and math assessments.

It is clear that these trends do not represent the wishes of parents. Last year, for example, University of Wisconsin professor Ken Goldstein reported that 64% of Wisconsin adults identify music as very or somewhat important when it comes to schooling. The similar figures for foreign-language instruction are 59%, and for physical education, 80%. It is not parents or the public, any more than it is the teachers, who are pushing schools to become gap-closing factories.

Of particular concern is the way "achievement-gap mania" has forced educators to quietly but systematically shortchange some students in the rush to serve others. Pollsters Farkas and Duffett, for instance, have reported that struggling students possess an unrivaled claim on teachers' attention. In 2008, the team found that 60% of teachers surveyed said that struggling students were a "top priority" at their schools while just 23% said the same of "academically advanced" students — even on a question to which teachers could provide multiple answers. When asked which students were most likely to get one-on-one attention from teachers, 80% of the survey participants said academically struggling students, while just 5% said academically advanced students.

Consider the case of Florida, which has been celebrated, especially by conservatives, for its success in closing racial achievement gaps. Mary Jane Tappen, Florida's deputy chancellor of education, has credited, in part, state policies that require any administrator or teacher who will have even *one* "English-language learner" in his school or class to sit through 60 hours of ELL-specific training. English teachers are required to receive *300 hours* of training in teaching

English as a second language. Clearly, those hundreds of hours of training consume dollars and time that can no longer be devoted to educating other children in subjects other than English as a second language.

The effects of achievement-gap mania have been particularly severe in the area of advanced instruction and gifted education. In February 2009, the California Legislature adopted a plan that allows public schools to divert state money for gifted children to "any educational purpose." A 2010 study by the California Legislative Analyst's Office found that 68% of the 231 school districts surveyed had shifted resources away from education for gifted students. California's Evergreen School District, for example, responded by eliminating all its programs for approximately 800 gifted children. After noting the extensive cuts being made to gifted and talented programs, the *San Francisco Chronicle* observed: "Critics see courses tailored for exceptional students as elitist and not much of an issue when compared with the vast number of students who are lagging grades behind their peers or dropping out of school."

Frank C. Worrell, faculty director of the Academic Talent Development Program at the University of California, Berkeley, has identified part of the problem with this approach. "We have focused on bringing up the bottom," he explains. "But we have failed to recognize that by ignoring the top, we are creating another problem. We are not sparking the creativity of those who have the most potential to make outstanding contributions."

Of course, advocates of the gap-closing agenda have not presented their cause in these terms. They do not tell schools to ignore white or affluent students, or non-tested subjects — they merely call for a focus on achievement gaps and insist on ignoring the downsides to doing so. Education Trust vice president Amy Wilkins has rejected the notion that there may be a tradeoff between universality and rigor, declaring it a "false choice." But the evidence suggests it is a very real choice, and one with grave implications for American education.

EDUCATION'S NEW LOSERS

It should be obvious that the United States cannot afford to be cavalier about the education of its best-performing students. Stanford University's Eric Hanushek, Harvard University's Paul Peterson, and the University of Munich's Ludger

Woessmann reported earlier this year that the share of American students who are accomplished in math trails those of most other industrialized nations. In 2006, 30 of the 56 nations participating in the Program for International Student Assessment math test had a larger percentage of students scoring at the international equivalent of the advanced level on our own National Assessment of Educational Progress tests than we did. On the 2007 Trends in International Math and Science Study, just 6% of American eighth graders scored "advanced." In Taiwan, Hong Kong, South Korea, and Finland, however, the proportion of students achieving at the same level was at least three times as large. Another dozen nations had at least twice as large a share of advanced students.

A universal and exclusive focus on low-achieving kids ignores the fact that different education strategies work best for different kinds of students. Earlier this year, the Fordham Institute's Mike Petrilli — a former Bush-administration official and NCLB champion who has since expressed concerns about the law — observed: "The question of whether affluent and disadvantaged kids need a different kind of education — different instructional strategies, different curriculum, maybe even different kinds of teachers — is a serious one. This discussion is easily demagogued . . . . But it's not racist to say that poor kids — who generally come to school with much less vocabulary, exposure to print, and much else — might need something different — more intense, more structured — than their well-off, better-prepared peers."

Before they even enter the classroom, many children from low-income and minority households are at a distinct educational disadvantage. Research demonstrates that children from more educated families tend to start school with much larger vocabularies, more exposure to the written word, more time having been read to, and more of the habits that make for a responsible, successful student. Kindergarteners from low-income households typically have a vocabulary of about 5,000 words, compared to the typical 20,000-word vocabulary of their more advantaged peers. The disparity results, in part, from the fact that many low-income children don't attend pre-school; low-income parents speak to their children about one-third as much as parents who are professionals; low-income parents read to their children much less than do other parents; and low-income children watch much more television than do their peers.

The implication is that, from the very beginning, disadvantaged and advantaged children have different educational needs and stand to benefit from different kinds of instruction. The kinds of teaching and support that can help disadvantaged students acquire the skills and knowledge that they did not receive at home are often superfluous or inappropriate for more advantaged children. In this way, gap-closing can transform from a strategy that lifts up the least proficient students into one that slows up the most proficient.

And children who are ready for new intellectual challenges pay a price when they sit in classrooms focused on their less proficient peers. In 2008, Brookings Institution scholar Tom Loveless reported that, while the nation's lowest-achieving students made significant gains in fourth-grade reading and math scores from 2000 to 2007, top students made anemic gains. Loveless found that students who comprised the bottom 10% of achievers saw visible progress in fourth-grade reading and math and eighth-grade math after 2000, but that the performance of students in the top decile barely moved. He concluded, "It would be a mistake to allow the narrowing of test score gaps, although an important accomplishment, to overshadow the languid performance trends of high-achieving students . . . .Gaps are narrowing because the gains of low-achieving students are outstripping those of high achievers by a factor of two or three to one."

Loveless's findings echo other research. A 1996 RAND Corporation study found that, when low-achieving students were placed in mixed-ability classrooms, they did about five percentage points better. High-achieving students, however, fared six percentage points *worse* in such classes — and middle-achieving students fared two percentage points worse than they did when placed in "tracked" classes. Weighing these effects out, the authors concluded that switching to mixed-ability classes in math would reduce aggregate achievement by 2%.

There is, of course, the occasional extraordinary teacher who can make heterogeneous classes work for all students. But such teachers are the exception, not the rule. Value-added testing guru Bill Sanders has reported, based on Tennessee achievement data, that high-scoring students made adequate gains only with the top 20% of teachers. Students at lower achievement levels, however, made progress with all but the least effective teachers. In other words, Sanders's research suggests that teacher quality may matter more for high-performing students than for their peers.

As with so much of the "achievement gap" agenda, mixed-ability instruction is not a bad idea per se. But it does impose costs. The gap-closing gospel holds that there should be no winners and losers in American education, but in practice it simply creates a different set of winners and losers.

THE DELUSION OF RIGOR

The cost of the relentless focus on gap-closing is perhaps most evident when it comes to advanced instruction, particularly Advanced Placement courses. Pressure to close gaps has meant pushing more disadvantaged students into AP courses, even when it has compromised rigor or standards.

Nationally, the number of high-school graduates who had taken at least one AP exam rose from 1 million in 2003 to 1.6 million in 2008. Enthusiasts argue that such expansion entails no downsides, and that enrolling more students in advanced classes doesn't dilute instructional quality. Unfortunately, the nation's AP teachers tell a different story. In a 2009 study, education pollsters Duffett and Farkas noted that just 14% of AP teachers believed that the growth in AP enrollment was caused by growth in the pool of qualified students. Sixty-five percent, meanwhile, said their school's policy was to encourage as many students as possible to take AP courses and exams, regardless of qualification. Indeed, just 29% said their school limited access to AP via prerequisites such as maintaining a minimum grade point average or obtaining teacher approval. Duffett and Farkas reported that this phenomenon was most evident in high-poverty schools, where 34% of AP teachers believed "administrators [were] pushing unqualified minority or low-income students into AP" and 50% said that their African-American and Hispanic students were not adequately prepared for AP instruction.

The result? Fifty-six percent of the AP teachers surveyed said that too many students were in over their heads; 39% reported that the aptitude of AP students and their capacity to do the work had declined, while just 16% said it had improved. And the College Board, the organization that administers the AP program, reports that the share of AP exams receiving the minimum passing score of 3 or better declined by four percentage points between 2003 and 2008.

This is hardly the first time that well-intentioned efforts to universalize access to high-caliber instruction have had troublesome consequences. American

Enterprise Institute scholar Mark Schneider, formerly the commissioner of the National Center for Education Statistics, has concluded that decades of efforts to boost the number of students taking rigorous math classes has caused a substantial dilution of those courses. Schneider has noted that the average number of math credits completed by a high-school graduate rose from 3.2 to 3.8 between 1990 and 2005, and that average math GPAs rose over that time from 2.2 to 2.6. While only a third of students completed algebra II in 1978, more than half did in 2008. And yet NAEP scores for students in algebra I, geometry, and algebra II were higher in 1978 than in 2008. In other words, more students were taking more advanced math and getting better grades — and yet our students knew less in 2008 than they did 30 years earlier. Schneider terms this phenomenon the "delusion of rigor."

There can be unfortunate, if often unacknowledged, consequences when we seek to universalize excellence. Such efforts can dilute instructional quality, make it tougher for teachers to go as deep or as fast as they otherwise might, and distract attention from advanced students. Given these mixed results, how did the gap-closing gospel become the organizing principle of American schooling?

HOW WE GOT HERE

Historically, there has been a tension between efforts to bolster the performance of elite students and efforts to promote educational equality. Despite cheerful assurances that the two are complementary, the ascendance of one tends to undermine and distract from the other. For example, the post-Sputnik National Defense Education Act of 1958 made a dramatic investment in high-achieving students in math, science, and language, but overlooked lower-performing students. Concerns about this disparity eventually led to the passage of the Elementary and Secondary Education Act of 1965 — a law that took the equality agenda of the Great Society and projected it onto America's K-12 schools.

But the ESEA failed to seriously advance the cause of educational equality. And in the years following its passage, the field of education policy stagnated, largely because of the influence of social scientists and education leaders convinced that schools could only minimally alter educational outcomes.

This glum view was fostered by sociologist James Coleman's 1966 study examining the first large-scale collection of data on school characteristics and student achievement. The Coleman Report concluded that parents' involvement in their children's lives had a vastly greater effect on achievement and eventual success than schooling did. Coleman's findings were reinforced in the 1970s by sociologist Christopher Jencks and a team at Harvard, who conducted an extensive re-analysis of the data and concluded that the influence of schooling was "marginal." Children, they argued, were affected far more by "what happens at home [and also perhaps] by what happens on the streets and by what they see on television. "The outcomes of schooling, Jencks and his team reported, depended almost entirely on "the characteristics of the entering children. Everything else — the school budget, its policies, the characteristics of the teachers — is either secondary or completely irrelevant."

These discouraging conclusions set the stage for decades of lackluster education policy, in which educators excused disappointing results by blaming circumstances beyond their control. The result, in the 1980s and then increasingly in the 1990s, was frustration among policymakers and would-be reformers. Reformers on both the left and the right conceded that a child's material, family, and community circumstances surely mattered, but decided to reject outright the notion that zip codes should determine academic success.

These critiques prompted a determination to help schools do a better job of serving students who were too often passed over or ignored. In theory, this should have been a healthy development; in practice, however, a sensible impulse became badly distorted. The result was the No Child Left Behind Act, to which much of today's achievement-gap mania can be traced. It was NCLB, after all, whose very title formally proclaimed the law "[a]n act to close the achievement gap."

To be fair, some reform like the No Child Left Behind Act was probably inevitable. For too long, inadequate instruction in essential skills and abysmal performance by poor, black, and Latino children had been tacitly accepted as the status quo. NCLB was thus largely the product of frustration. It was crafted by Washington policymakers fed up with the seeming refusal of educators to accept responsibility for persistent mediocrity. And in spring 2001, with strong bipartisan support, NCLB passed the House of Representatives by a vote of 381 to 41 and the Senate by a vote of 87 to 10.

G-10

America got the particular reform law that it did, though, because George W. Bush ran in 2000 as a "compassionate conservative." Eager to showcase his compassion, he drew upon his record as an education reformer in Texas to make the case for educational accountability. But testing, standards, and accountability alone could too easily come across as heartless, especially for a Republican trying to assuage moderate voters. Thus Bush decided to speak not merely of accountability; he also pledged to "leave no child behind." As Bush strategist Karl Rove explained in his book *Courage and Consequence*: "When Bush said education was the civil rights struggle of our time or that the absence of an accountability system in our schools meant black, brown, poor, and rural children were getting left behind, it gave listeners important information about his respect and concern for every family and deepened the impression that he was a different kind of Republican whom suburban voters . . . could be proud to support."

That pledge provided much common ground between Bush and congressional warhorses Ted Kennedy (ranking Democrat on the Senate education committee) and George Miller (ranking Democrat on the House education committee). And in negotiations with Kennedy, Miller, and other liberal allies, Bush's team embraced a bill that featured all kinds of "achievement gap" requirements that had been absent from the president's original blueprint. They agreed that states would be required to "disaggregate" test scores by race and income, so that schools and districts could be judged on the performance of individual groups. And all parties agreed that school performance should be judged not by how well the schools did as a whole, but rather by achievement on reading and math assessments of the school's worst-performing demographic "subgroup." In other words, every public school in America would henceforth be judged primarily on its ability to drive up the reading and math scores of its most disadvantaged students. Indeed, as Bush's NCLB blueprint proposed, "Sanctions [would] be based on a state's failure to narrow the achievement gap . . . in math and reading in grades 3 through 8."

In essence, NCLB was an effort to link "conservative" nostrums of accountability to Great Society notions of "social justice." The result was a noble exercise hailed for its compassion. The sad truth, however, is that the whole achievement-gap enterprise has been bad for schooling, bad for most children, and bad for the nation.

A COUNTERPRODUCTIVE CAMPAIGN

At first, it may seem counterintuitive to suggest that a massive, well-intentioned education-reform effort — supported on both sides of the political aisle, by major philanthropic foundations, and by some prominent voices in the civil-rights community — could be anything other than a blessing for American education. And yet five major consequences of NCLB, and of the achievement-gap mania it helped to spawn, demonstrate how this approach has ultimately been harmful to American education.

First, achievement-gap mania has signaled to the vast majority of American parents that school reform isn't about *their* kids. They are now expected to support efforts to close the achievement gap simply because it's "the right thing to do," regardless of the implications for their own children's education. In fact, given that only about one household in five even contains school-age children — and given that two-thirds of families with children do not live in underserved urban neighborhoods, or do not send their kids to public schools, or otherwise do not stand to benefit from the gap-closing agenda — the result is a tiny potential constituency for achievement-gap reform, made up of perhaps 6% or 7% of American households.

Because middle-class parents and suburbanites have no personal stake in the gap-closing enterprise, reforms are tolerated rather than embraced. The most recent annual Gallup poll on attitudes toward schooling reported that just 20% of respondents said "improving the nation's lowest-performing schools" was the most important of the nation's education challenges. Indeed, while just 18% of the public gave American schools overall an A or a B, a sizable majority thought their own elementary and middle schools deserved those high grades. The implication is that most Americans, even those with school-age children, currently see education reform as time and money spent on other people's children. This makes school reform a losing vote for suburban legislators — one that they can take because it's the right thing to do, but that is calculated to burn rather than win political capital. The focus on achievement gaps makes for bad politics by making it hard to build broad, sustained support for reform.

Second, achievement-gap mania has created a dangerous complacency, giving suburban and middle-class Americans the false sense that things are just fine in their own schools. Thus it's no surprise that professionals and suburbanites tend to regard "reforms" — from merit pay to charter schooling — as measures that they'll tolerate as long as they're reserved for urban schools, but that they won't stand for in their own communities. As liberal blogger Matt Yglesias has noted, "Apocalyptic talk about 'failing' schools and intense elite focus on the problems of the least-privileged students tends to obscure the more banal reality that most schools are non-optimal in lots of ways." He elaborates:

> An exaggerated view of how terrible "the public schools" are goes hand in hand with exaggerated complacency about one's own local school. If you walked around thinking that the average American male was 5'3" then you'd also walk around thinking that you and your friends and neighbors are really tall. It would actually be more politically useful to have people more focused on the modest but real problems in their own local schools than have them morbidly obsessed with semi-mythical tales of a "broken" school system that they're fortunate not to be stuck in.

The truth is that even the nation's better-performing schools operate under an anachronistic model of schooling that could stand some sensible reforms. And yet because achievement-gap mania has distilled "education reform" to measures that raise the test scores of poor and minority students, the solutions to what ails American education more broadly simply aren't being developed — in part because the question is hardly ever asked.

Gap-closing strategies can be downright unhelpful or counterproductive when it comes to serving most students and families, and so can turn them off to education reform altogether. Longer school years and longer school days can be terrific for disadvantaged students or low achievers, but may be a recipe for backlash if imposed on families who already offer their kids many summer opportunities and extracurricular activities. Policies that seek to shift the "best" teachers to schools and classrooms serving low-achieving children represent a frontal assault on middle-class and affluent families. And responding to such concerns by belittling them is a sure-fire strategy for ensuring that school reform never amounts to more than a self-righteous crusade at odds with the interests of most middle-class families.

Third, achievement-gap mania has prompted reformers to treat schools as instruments to be used in crafting desired social outcomes, capable of being "fixed" simply through legislative solutions and federal policies. This tendency is hardly surprising, given that most of the thinking about achievement gaps is done in the context not of education reform but of "social justice." Thus gap-closers approach the challenge not as educators but as social engineers, determined to see schools fix the problems that job-training initiatives, urban redevelopment, income supports, and a slew of other well-intentioned government welfare programs have failed to address.

With the social engineer's calm assurance that there are clear, identifiable interventions to resolve every problem, today's education reformers insist that closing the achievement gap is a simple matter of identifying "what works" and then requiring schools to do it. And integral to determining "what works" has been evaluating different strategies in terms of their effects on reading and math scores and graduation rates. This approach has been especially popular when it comes to identifying good teachers. But while the ability to move these scores may be 90% of the job for an elementary-school teacher in Philadelphia or Detroit, it doesn't necessarily make sense to use these metrics to evaluate teachers in higher-performing schools — where most children easily clear the literacy and numeracy bar, and where parents are more concerned with how well teachers develop their children's other skills and talents.

Teacher evaluation and pay systems based on gap-closing make little or no allowance for such considerations. One result is that most of the public, rightly or wrongly, puts more stock in its own perceptions than in NCLB-style accountability measurements. For instance, Gallup has reported that, when asked how they would interpret the fact that "large numbers of public schools fail to meet the requirements established by the NCLB law," just 43% of respondents said they'd blame the public schools for the outcome. Forty-nine percent, meanwhile, said they would be more likely to blame "the law itself." Thus, in a roundabout way, NCLB has undermined its own legitimacy among the voting public; for this, it has the school-reformers-turned-social-engineers to thank.

Fourth, the achievement-gap mindset stifles innovation. When a nation focuses all its energies on boosting the reading and math scores of the most vulnerable students, there is neither much cause nor much appetite for developing and pursuing education strategies capable of improving American schools overall.

Consider the case of school choice. Today, for all the vague talk of innovation, charter schools and school vouchers rarely do more than allow poor, urban students to move from unsafe, horrific schools into better conventional-looking schools. The leading brands in charter schooling, for instance, almost uniformly feature traditional classrooms; an extended school day, school year, or both; and a reliance on directive pedagogy attuned to the needs of disadvantaged students. In other words, these are terrific 19th-century schools. One has to search long and hard among the nation's more than 5,000 charter schools to find the handful that are experimenting with labor-saving technologies, technology-infused instruction, or new staffing models better suited to the 21st century.

Furthermore, the intense focus on gap-closing has led to a notion of "innovation" dedicated almost entirely to driving up math and reading scores and graduation rates for low-income and minority students. Promising innovations that promote science, foreign-language learning, or musical instruction have garnered little public investment or acclaim. Even in terms of math and reading, there is not much interest in interventions that do not show up on standardized state assessments. The Obama administration's $650 million Investing in Innovation Fund — designed to spur investments in innovative educational providers and practices — specified that applicants needed to "demonstrate their previous success in closing achievement gaps, improving student progress toward proficiency, increasing graduation rates, or recruiting and retaining high-quality teachers and principals." There is, of course, considerable merit to such a focus. But one undeniable consequence is that it has dramatically narrowed the scope of education research and development — to the inevitable detriment of the nation's schools.

Fifth, in a terrible irony, achievement-gap mania has indirectly made it more difficult for reformers to promote integrated schools. Philanthropic foundations that support education causes are interested in serving as many poor and minority children as possible; when 30% to 40% of a student body is made up of white or affluent students, the school is deemed suspect, as reform-minded foundations see such programs as "wasting" a third of their seats. Bragging rights go to charter schools or programs that have the highest-octane mix of poor and minority kids. The upshot is that it is terribly difficult to generate interest in nurturing racially or socioeconomically integrated schools, even though just about every observer thinks that more such schools would be good for kids, communities, and the country.

REKINDLING THE DEBATE

Perhaps the greatest irony surrounding achievement-gap mania is that, for a reform approach ultimately rooted in a moral claim, its moral philosophy is not all that compelling.

If anyone could be considered the patron saint of gap-closing, it is 20th-century philosopher John Rawls. Rawls authored the landmark treatise _A Theory of Justice_, which argued that a just society should ensure, according to the "difference principle," that any social and economic inequalities are arranged for the benefit of society's least advantaged group. This would seem to be a clear justification for shortchanging most students in order to focus on those at the bottom.

And yet even Rawls's view was far more nuanced than that of today's gap-closers. Indeed, Rawls cautioned:

> Now the difference principle . . . does not require society to try to even out handicaps as if all were expected to compete on a fair basis in the same race. But the difference principle would allocate resources in education, say, so as to improve the long-term expectation of the least favored. If this end is attained by giving more attention to the better endowed, it is permissible; otherwise not.

It would be comforting if gap-closers even occasionally took seriously Rawls's warning that "it is not in general to the advantage of the less fortunate to propose policies which reduce the talents of others." Instead, they dismiss such concerns with moral indignation or specious claims that their preferred remedies entail no tradeoffs. In doing so, they duck the unpleasant reality that we cannot do everything: Doubling down on one area of education reform inevitably means easing up somewhere else.

All children in a free nation have a moral claim to attend schools that will help them discover and develop their gifts. And while difficult choices must always be made, we should be wary of shaping schools in ways that explicitly favor some of our children while shortchanging others. It is long past time for a more mature approach to education reform — one that recognizes that there are no silver bullets or one-size-fits-all solutions, and that fixing what ails America's schools will not always be easy or obvious. Decisions about how much to focus on this child versus that child *should* be painful enough that we don't make them cavalierly. And in making these difficult decisions, responsible people of good faith can and will disagree.

The problem with achievement-gap mania is not that it is necessarily wrong; the problem is that its self-confident purveyors have been uniformly uninterested in the cost, complications, or consequences of their crusade. The result has been to effectively stifle debate, alienate most parents from the school-reform agenda, and insist that a flawed, mechanistic vision of schooling ought to steer our course in the 21st century.

The response to this problem cannot be to dispute the moral claims of our most vulnerable children. Rather, the solution is to ensure that these claims are placed in their proper context — weighed against the competing claims of other children and of society at large. The obligation of serious reformers, then, is to rekindle the debate. They have a responsibility to help lawmakers, educators, and foundations understand that, while achievement gaps are important, they are just one challenge in a vast education landscape. Reformers must insist that the demands of gap-closing crusaders be subjected to rigorous, careful scrutiny. And they must re-open the world of education policy to fresh ways of envisioning what American schooling can be.

Only then will we be able to move beyond No Child Left Behind and the frustrations and failures that have followed. In the end, deciding that school is the place where we teach poor children to read and do math — and that everyone else will be left alone to figure out the rest — seems an impoverished and ultimately self-defeating agenda for education reform in the 21st century.

Frederick M. Hess is director of education-policy studies at the American Enterprise Institute and author of The Same Thing Over and Over: How School Reformers Get Stuck in Yesterday's Ideas. *This essay was made possible in part by generous support from the Hertog/Simon Fund for Policy Analysis.*

PARENTS GROUP HITS BACK AT BILLIONAIRE BROAD'S INFLUENCE ON EDUCATION

A national parent group is attacking the influence of LA billionaire Eli Broad's influence on public education, a reach that extends into Denver with the controversial non-educator Superintendent of Denver Public Schools, Tom Boasberg. Parents across America have published this parent's guide to the influence of the Broad Foundation:

The question I ask is why should Eli Broad and Bill Gates have more of a say as to what goes on in my child's classroom than I do? – Sue Peters, Seattle parent

In recent months, three prominent school district superintendents have resigned, after allegations of mismanagement, autocratic leadership styles, and/or the pursuit of unpopular policies. All three were trained by the Broad Superintendents Academy: Maria Goodloe-Johnson (class of 2003) of the Seattle school district, LaVonne Sheffield (class of 2002) of the Rockford, Illinois school district, and Jean-Claude Brizard (class of 2008) of the Rochester New York school district. Brizard resigned to take the job as CEO of Chicago schools, but his superintendency in Rochester had been mired in controversy. Another Broad-trained Superintendent recently announced his resignation: Tom Brady (class of 2004) of Providence, Rhode Island.

Three more Broad-trainees have been recently placed in new positions of authority: John Deasy (class of 2006), as Superintendent of the Los Angeles United School District, John White (class of 2010), Superintendent of the Recovery School District in New Orleans, and Chris Cerf (class of 2004), New Jersey's Acting Education Commissioner. Tom Boasberg was appointed Denver's Superintendent in January 2009,  shortly after taking an "Intensive" training at the Broad Academy. (See map from the Broad website, showing where until recently their trainees served.)

This summary is designed to help parents and other concerned citizens better understand the Broad Foundation's role in training new superintendents and other "reform" activities, and how the foundation leverages its wealth to impose a top-down, corporate-style business model on our public schools. It is time for communities to become aware of how this major force works.

What is the Broad Foundation?

The Edythe and Eli Broad Foundation engages in venture philanthropy in four areas: education, medical research, contemporary art, and civic projects in Los Angeles. The foundation was established in 1999 by billionaire Eli Broad (b. 1933) who made his fortune in real estate and the insurance business.

A closer look at the Broad Foundation's "investment" in education

The Gates Foundation, the Walton Family Foundation, and the Broad Foundation form a powerful triumvirate. The combined net worth of the three families who operate these foundations is $152 billion. By strategically deploying their immense wealth through training school leaders, financing think-tank reports, and supporting "Astro Turf" advocacy groups, these three foundations have been able to steer the direction of education reform over the past decade.

The Broad Foundation is the least wealthy of the three, but has still spent nearly $400 million on its mission of "transforming urban K-12 public education through better governance, management, labor relations and competition." *But what does that actually mean?*

The signature effort of the Broad Foundation is its investment in its training programs, operated through the Broad Center for the Management of School Systems and the Broad Institute for School Boards. The Broad Center for the Management of School Systems is the larger of the two and consists of two programs: the Broad Superintendents Academy and the Broad Residency in Urban Education.

The Broad Superintendents Academy runs a training program held during six weekends over ten months, after which graduates are placed in large districts as superintendents. Those accepted into the program ("Broad Fellows") are not required to have a background in-education; many come instead from careers in the military, business, or government. Tuition and travel expenses for participants are paid for by the Broad Center, which also sometimes covers a share of the graduates' salaries when they are appointed into district leadership positions. The foundation's website boasts that 43 percent of all large urban superintendent openings were filled by Broad Academy graduates in 2009.

The Broad Superintendents Academy's weekend training course provides an "alternative" certification process which has come to supplant or override the typical regulations in many states that require that individuals have years of experience as a teacher and principal before being installed as a school district superintendents.

The Broad Residency in Urban Education is a two-year program, during which individuals with MBAs, JDs, etc. in the early stages of their careers are placed in high-level managerial positions in school districts, charter management organizations, or state and federal departments of education. The Broad Center subsidizes approximately 33 percent of each Resident's salary.

For financially struggling school districts, the Broad Foundation's offer of trained personnel or services for a free or reduced cost is extremely appealing, and creates a "pipeline" of individuals with the same ideology who can be installed in central office positions.

The Broad Institute for School Boards provides three training programs for elected school board members and non-Broad-trained superintendents conducted in partnership with the Center for Reform of School Systems (CRSS). The Institute trains new board members at a one-week summer residential setting. Its Alumni Institute is an advanced course for experienced school board members. The third program, Reform Governance in Action, is by invitation only and provides "a long-term, training/consulting partnership program to selected large, urban districts." The Broad Foundation underwrites 80 percent of all program costs through a grant to CRSS.

The "Broad Prize for Education" is an annual monetary award which is designated for college scholarships; it is given to the urban school district which the foundation deems as the most "improved" in the country. The selection process is sometimes seen as more political than based on actual results.

H-3

The Broad Foundation also supports a broad range of pro-charter school advocacy groups, as well as alternative training programs for non-educators who want to work as teachers and principals (Teach for America, New Leaders for New Schools).

In addition, the foundation offers free diagnostic "audits" to school districts, along with recommendations aligned with its policy preferences. It produces a number of guides and toolkits for school districts, including a "School Closure Guide," based on the experiences of Broad-trained administrators involved in closing schools in Boston, Charleston, Chicago, Dallas, Washington, D.C., Miami-Dade County, Oakland, Pittsburgh, St. Louis, and Seattle.

The foundation finances the Education Innovation Laboratory, run by Harvard economist Roland Fryer, which carries out large-scale experiments in schools districts, focused on teacher pay for performance and rewarding students for good test scores and grades. So far, these trials have failed to demonstrate positive results.

The foundation provided start-up funding for Parent Revolution (formerly the Los Angeles Parent Union), the group which developed the "Parent Trigger" legislation, designed to encourage the conversion of public schools to charter schools. Broad has also has given large amounts of money to Education Reform Now, a pro-charter school advocacy organization.

Eli Broad has said he "expects to be a major contributor" to Students First, former D.C. Chancellor Michelle Rhee's organization that advocates for the expansion of charters, vouchers, and an end to seniority protections for teachers. And journalist Richard Whitmire, author of "The Bee Eater," an admiring biography of Rhee, expressed his gratitude in the book to Democrats for Education Reform, a pro-charter lobbying organization, for serving as the "pass through" for funds from the Broad Foundation which allowed him to "invest everything in book research."

The foundation provided start-up funds to New York City's Leadership Academy, which trains individuals to serve as principals in the city public schools, several of whose graduates have been accused of financial misconduct, as well as arbitrary and dictatorial treatment of teachers, students and parents.

The foundation also helps sponsors media events (a PBS series on the "education crisis" hosted by Charlie Rose, the series Education Nation on NBC, etc.). These programs help promote for Eli Broad's vision of free-market education reform.

In addition to using his foundation to effect change to American public education, Eli Broad has made personal campaign contributions to candidates who are favourably disposed to his preferred policies, even down to the local school board level. In this way, he has helped influence the selection of superintendents who are aligned with him ideologically, even though they may not be Broad Academy graduates.

For instance, Broad contributed to the campaigns of school board candidates who supported former U.S. Assistant Attorney General Alan Bersin's appointment as superintendent of San Diego's school district. A 2006 Vanity Fair article by Bob Colacello reported that "Broad believes reform must come "the top down" and that his foundation "plans to virtually take over the Delaware school system in 2007, pending approval from that state's legislature."

In 2003, Joseph Wise (class of 2003) was installed as superintendent of Christina School District, Delaware's largest. In 2006, Wise was succeeded by Lillian Lowery (class of 2004), who served until 2009 when she was appointed as the state's Secretary of Education. Two Broad Residents work under Lowery at the state level. Another Broad superintendent, Marcia Lyles (class of 2006), replaced Lowery as superintendent of Christina School District.

Along with Bill Gates, Broad contributed millions of dollars to the campaign to extend mayoral control of the public schools in New York City under Michael Bloomberg. Among the leaders he is close to and has personally advised behind the scenes are former NYC Chancellor Joel Klein, former D.C. Chancellor Michelle Rhee, AFT President Randi Weingarten, and US Secretary of Education Arne Duncan.

How the Broad Foundation affects public school families

Broad and his foundation believe that public schools should be run like a business. One of the tenets of his philosophy is to produce system change by "investing in a disruptive force." Continual reorganizations, firings of staff, and experimentation to create chaos or "churn" is believed to be productive and beneficial, as it weakens the ability of communities to resist change.

As Jack Welch, former CEO of General Electric, a proponent of this philosophy has said, *"...we can afford to make lots more mistakes and in fact we have to throw more things at the wall. The big companies that get into trouble are those that try to manage their size instead of experimenting with it."*

A hallmark of the Broad-style leadership is closing existing schools rather than attempting to improve them, increasing class size, opening charter schools, imposing high-stakes test-based accountability systems on teachers and students, and implementing of pay for performance schemes. The brusque and often punitive management style of Broad-trained leaders has frequently alienated parents and teachers and sparked protests.

Several communities have forced their Broad-trained superintendents to resign, including Arnold "Woody" Carter (class or 2002), formerly of the Capistrano Unified School District; Thandiwee Peebles,(class of 2002), formerly of the Minneapolis Public School District; and John Q. Porter (class of 2006), formerly of the Oklahoma City Public School District.

A number of other Broad-trained superintendents have received votes of "no confidence" from the teachers in their districts, including Rochester's Jean-Claude Brizard (class of 2008), Seattle's Maria Goodloe-Johnson (class of 2003); Deborah Sims (class of 2005) while Superintendent of the Antioch Unified School District (CA); Matthew Malone (class of 2003) while Superintendent of the Swampscott School District (MA); and most recently,Melinda J. Boone (class of 2004) Superintendent of the Worcester Public Schools (MA).

The Oakland Unified School District (CA) experienced a series of three consecutive Broad-trained, state-appointed administrators over a period of six years. The first, Randolph Ward (class of 2003), aroused huge protests with his plans to close schools and even hired a personal bodyguard for the duration of his tenure. Ward was followed by Kimberly Statham (class of 2003), and Vincent Mathews (class of 2006), all of whom left the district in financial shambles. A civil grand jury found that

"....the district was hampered by continuous staff turnover, particularly in the area of finance, numerous reorganizations and a succession of state administrators...After nearly five years of state management, OUSD's budget remains unbalanced and the district's future is unclear."

H-6

Joseph Wise (class of 2003), formerly Superintendent of the Duval County Florida Public Schools, was found to have spent thousands of dollars on personal purchases while a superintendent in Delaware, before being fired by his Duval post in disgrace. While a finalist for the post of Superintendent in Washoe County in Nevada, Kimberly Olson (class of 2005) pled guilty of having engaged in war profiteering when she was a colonel in Iraq.

Chris Cerf (class of 2004), the acting New Jersey Education Commissioner, has been criticized for not identifying his involvement in a consulting firm which developed an secret plan to turn many Newark public schools over to charter operators. The Broad Foundation acknowledged that it put up $500,000 to pay for the plan. Deborah Gist (class of 2008), Rhode Island Commissioner of Education, has supported the firing of all teachers in Central Falls and more recently in Providence, and is aggressively fighting seniority protections for teachers.

General Anthony Tata (class of 2009), has been embroiled in controversy for dismantling Wake County's desegregation plan. John Covington (class of 2008), Superintendent of Kansas City Schools, has announced his intention to close half the schools districts in the city. Robert Bobb (class of 2005), the Emergency Financial Manager of the Detroit Public Schools, recently sent layoff notices to every one of the district's 5,466 salaried employees, including all its teachers, and said that nearly a third of the district's schools_would be closed or turned over to private charter operators. At a recent town hall which Bobb had called so he could go over his plan, angry students, parents, and teachers drove him from the meeting. He was escorted out by his six bodyguards.

Conclusion

Eli Broad is a wealthy individual, accountable to no one but himself, who wields vast power over our public schools. Parents and community members should be aware of the extent to which the he and his foundation influence educational policies in districts throughout the country, through Broad-funded advocacy groups, Broad-sponsored experiments and reports, and the placement of Broad-trained school leaders, administrators and superintendents.

Parents Across America considers Broad's influence to be inherently undemocratic, as it disenfranchises parents and other stakeholders in an effort to privatize our public schools and imposes corporate-style policies without our

H-7

consent. We strongly oppose allowing our nation's education policy to be driven by billionaires who have no education expertise, who do not send their own children to public schools, and whose particular biases and policy preferences are damaging our children's ability to receive a quality education.

Maps showing where some of the Broad superintendents and residents are currently employed can be found on the Broad Foundation's website: Broad Superintendents Academy Fellows and Broad Residents, as well as links to more information about them.

The only complete list of Broad Superintendent trainees is on The Broad Report website, which was created by Sharon Higgins, a founding member of Parents Across America.

Appendix I

American Association of Community Colleges / NCHE Fast Facts About Community College

Number and type of colleges

Public	986
Independent	115
Tribal	31
Total	1,132

Headcount Enrollment (fall 2009)					
By program type	#	%	By attendance	#	%
Credit	8M	61.5%	Part-time	7.54 M	58%
Noncredit	5M	38.5%	Full-time	5.46M	42%
Total	13 M				
Estimated increase fall 2009-fall 2011: 2.9%					

Student Demographics					
Age		Gender		Ethnicity	
Average	28	Women	57%	White	54%
Median	23	Men	43%	Hispanic	16%
< 21	39%			Black	14%
22-39	45%			Asian/Pacific Islander	6%

	1			
40+	5%		Native American	1%
			Other/unknown	10%

Other significant demographics:

First generation to attend college 42%

Single parents	13%
Non–U.S. citizens	6%
Veterans	3%
Students with disabilities	12%

Representation of Community College Students Among Undergraduates (fall 2009)	
% who are CC students	Undergraduate segment
44%	all U.S. undergraduates
43%	first-time freshmen
54%	Native American
51%	Hispanic
45%	Asian/Pacific Islander
44%	Black

Employment status (2007–2008)

Full-time students employed full time	21%
Full-time students employed part time	59%

Part-time students employed full time	40%
Part-time students employed part time	47%

Student financial aid (2007–2008)

% of students applying:	
Any aid	59%
Federal aid	42%

% of students receiving:	
Any aid	46%
Federal grants	21%
Federal loans	10%
State aid	13%
Institutional aid	11%

% of federal aid received by community colleges (2009–2010)

Pell Grants	32%
Campus-based aid	10%
Academic competitiveness grants	18%

Average Annual Tuition and Fees (2011–2012)

Community colleges (public, in district	$2,963
4-year colleges (public, in state)	$8,244

Degrees and Certificates Awarded (2008–2009)

Associate degrees	630,000
Certificates	425,000

Bachelor's degrees awarded by 48 public and 82 independent colleges Revenue Sources (2008–2009)

State funds	34%
Local funds	20%
Tuition and fees	16%
Federal funds	16%
Other	13%

RAISE THE COMMUNITY COLLEGE GRADUATION RATE

By the Monitor's Editorial Board / April 26, 2010

Roughly half of all those in college attend a community college, yet the graduation rate is dismal at these two-year schools. They must focus on student completion. Increasing the community college graduation rate is a matter of national competitiveness and job retraining.

'Tis the season for cap and gown, but at community colleges, many of the students won't graduate on time – or ever.

America's nearly 1,200 community colleges are the workhorses of higher education, allowing open access to all who desire to learn. Of all students in college, about 45 percent attend these institutions, which were designed for a fast, two-year time of study to earn an associate degree.

High unemployment and the cost of four-year colleges have spurred record enrollment at these schools – but they're failing to graduate students in high numbers and on time. About half will drop out before their second year. Only 25 percent finish in three years. Those who do graduate take an average of five years to complete their degrees.

Last summer, President Obama focused on these affordable colleges that disproportionately serve the poor, minorities, working adults, and parents. He correctly saw their potential to prepare people for a job market that increasingly demands a college degree. In keeping with his emphasis on education, Mr. Obama set a national goal of raising the number of community college graduates by 5 million by the end of the decade. And he pledged $12 billion to the effort.

It was an unprecedented promise to these schools, which are seeing their budgets cut by cash-strapped states just as students flood their campuses. For the first time, many community colleges are actually having to turn students away – or even offer courses late at night.

Unfortunately, Congress agreed to provide only $2 billion of the president's plan, mostly for job training – a traditional and needed role of community colleges. With long-term unemployment ahead, these colleges are critical to retraining America's workforce.

J-1

Admirably, to meet Obama's goal, the nation's community colleges have pledged to increase the graduation rate by 50 percent – even without the remaining $10 billion. Collectively, they appear ready to look beyond their traditional focus on "open access" to higher completion rates and educational results.

The colleges are also awakening to the need to collect data on what works and to make decisions based on their findings.

Change is percolating. A six-year-old privately funded effort, Achieving the Dream, is helping more than 100 community colleges use student-achievement data to guide new ways to increase graduations and transfers to four-year colleges.

Evidence shows that too many course choices can overwhelm a new student, as can traditional class schedules, which are not always geared toward work or parenting obligations. And the longer college study drags on, the less the likelihood of finishing. Sixty percent of students take remedial courses at community colleges, but they also get bogged down in these noncredit classes. Now colleges are looking at faster and more flexible formats for this extra help.

Congress should find a way to fund the rest of the money the president promised community colleges. Yes, these schools are primarily a local endeavor, but they serve the national interest in creating a competitive workforce. And like Obama's "race to the top" funding for public K-12 schools, the federal community college program was meant to encourage and reward innovative programs that work, so that they can be emulated across the country.

In the meantime, however, community colleges should continue to change their culture to a more results-oriented approach – a strategy that K-12 schools began years ago.

APPENDIX K

POVERTY IN THE U.S. BY THE NUMBERS: NPR

Poverty In The U.S. By The Numbers, appeared on the website www.npr.org July 10, 2012. Based on figures at from the 2010 Census: 2006-2010 American Community Survey Legal Momentum's "Reading Between the Lines: Women's Poverty in the United States, 2010" (Credit: Stephanie d'Otreppe, Nicole Cohen, JoElla Straley.NPR), the graphics spell out in graphic detail the stark reality of poverty in the U.S. Fifteen percent or 46.2 million Americans are in poverty, increasing from 2009 by 2.6 million. Establishing the fact that two in 10 people in the U.S. lives in poverty.

NATIONAL 2010 POVERTY RATE, **15.1%**

There were 46.2 million people in poverty, a 2.6 million increase from 2009 – the fourth consecutive annual U.S. were in poverty.

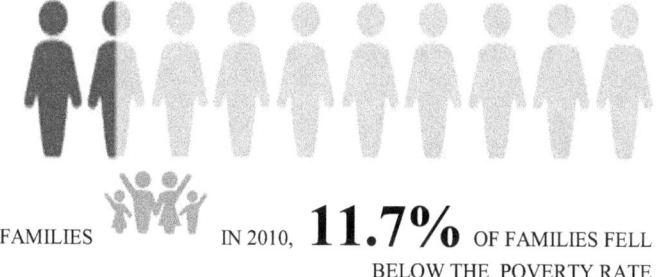

FAMILIES IN 2010, **11.7%** OF FAMILIES FELL BELOW THE POVERTY RATE

A family is counted as poor if its pretax money income is below its poverty threshold. Money income does not include noncash benefits such as public housing, Medicaid, employer-provided health insurance and food stamps.

K-1

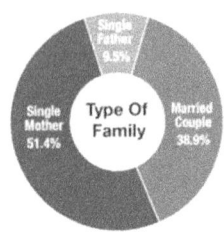

2010 POVERTY THRESHOLD

SINGLE INDIVIDUAL under 65 65 years & older
$11,344 $10,458

SINGLE PARENT one child two children three children
$15,030 $17,568 $22,190

TWO ADULTS   no children $14,602
one child two children three children
$17,552 $22,113 $26,023

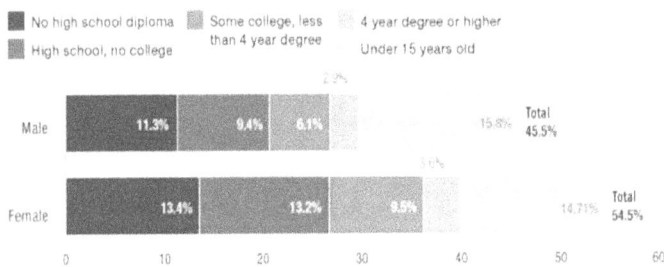

MALES AND FEMALES   IN 2010, WOMEN WERE **29%**
MORE LIKELY TO BE POOR THAN MEN

About one of every seven women was poor, compared to about one of every nine men.

BREAKDOWN OF PEOPLE IN POVERTY BY GENDER AND EDUCATION*

Women are more likely to be poor than men with the same level of education.

*Based on the highest grade completed. Applies only to people age 15 and older. People under 15 are included in totals only.

CHILDREN AND AGE
2010 CHILD POVERTY RATE,

21.6%

The 2010 child poverty rate was the highest since 2001. More than 1.1 million children were added to the poverty population between 2009 and 2010.

IN 2010, MORE THAN

1 IN 5

CHILDREN IN THE U.S. LIVED IN POVERTY

POVERTY RAGE BY AGE

Between 2009 and 2010, the poverty rate increased for children under age 18, by 1.3 percent, and people aged 18 to64, by 8 percent. There was no change for people aged 65 and older.

PERCENT OF CHILDREN IN THE UNITED STATES IN POVERTY IN 2010, BY RACE AND HISPANIC ORIGIN

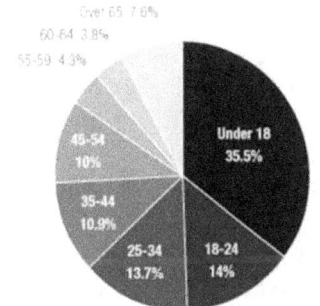

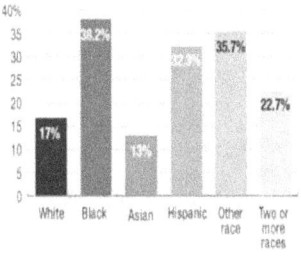

PERCENTAGE OF CHILDREN IN THE UNITED STATES IN POVERTY IN 2010, BY RACE AND HISPANIC ORIGIN

RACE AND ETHNICITY   The poverty rate for non-Hispanic whites was lower than the poverty rates for other racial groups. Between 2009 and 2010, Asians were the only racial group without a significant change or increase in poverty.

POVERTY RATE BY RACE   **MEDIAN INCOME BY RACE**

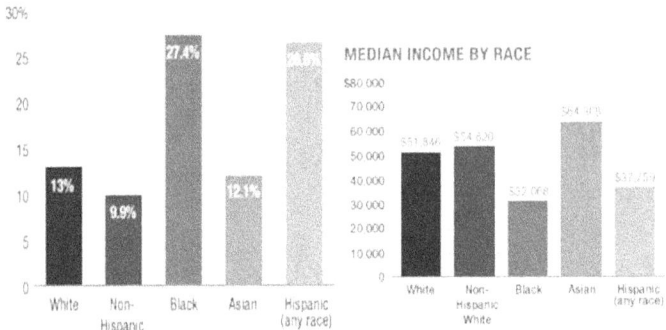

MEDIAN INCOME BY RACE

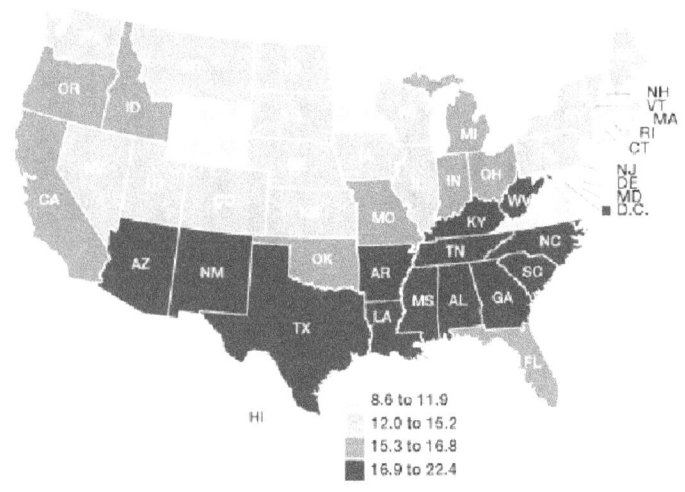

STATE BY STATE   **PERCENT IN POVERTY: 2010**

8.6 to 11.9
12.0 to 15.2
15.3 to 16.8
16.9 to 22.4

IN 2010,

Mississippi

was the poorest state in the nation.

POVERTY RATE	UNEMPLOYMENT*	MEDIAN INCOME
21.3%	**10.2%**	**$35,850**

New Hampshire

was the wealthiest state in the nation.

POVERTY RATE	UNEMPLOYMENT*	MEDIAN INCOME
6.6%	**5.6%**	**$66,707**

POOREST CITIES IN THE U.S.

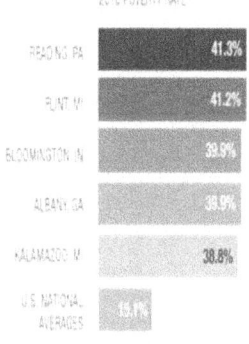
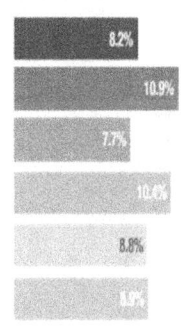
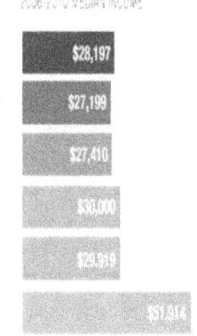

	2010 POVERTY RATE	2011 ANNUAL UNEMPLOYMENT*	2006-2010 MEDIAN INCOME
READING PA	41.3%	8.2%	$28,197
FLINT MI	41.2%	10.9%	$27,199
BLOOMINGTON IN	39.9%	7.7%	$27,410
ALBANY GA	38.9%	10.4%	$30,000
KALAMAZOO MI	38.8%	8.8%	$29,919
U.S. NATIONAL AVERAGES	15.1%	8.9%	$51,914

K-5

NUMBER IN POVERTY AND POVER RATE: 1959-2010

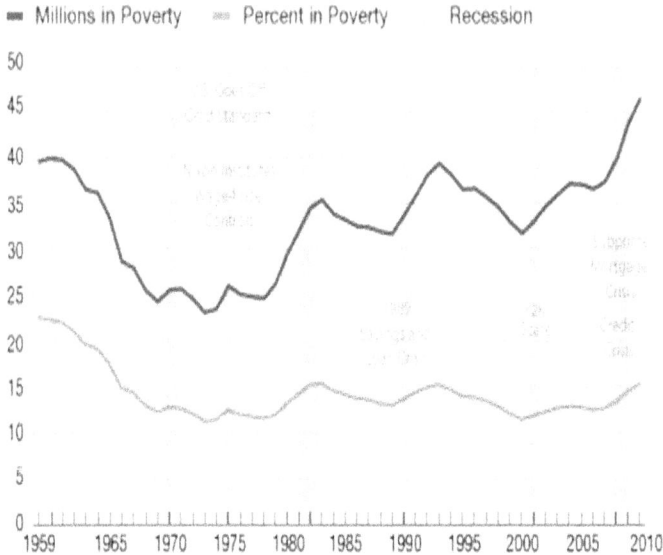

The poverty rate in 2010 was the highest poverty rate since 1993 but was 7.3 percent lower than the poverty rate in 1959, the first year for which poverty estimates are available.

Although the number of those in poverty has risen, the percentage of those in poverty has fallen by 7.4 percent since 1959,

Since it was first measured in 1959, the poverty rate has never been below 11 percent.

THE LOWEST POVERTY RATE WAS IN 1973 AT **11.1%**

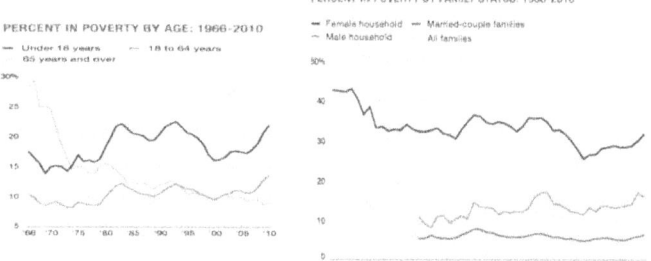

Source: 2010 Census, 2006-2010 American Community Survey, Legal Momentum's "Reading Between the Lines: Women's Poverty in the United States, 2010" Credit: Stephanie d'Otreppe, Nicole Cohen, JoElla Straley.NPR (online at http://www.npr.org/2012/07/10/156387172/poverty-in-the-u-s-by-the-numbers)

BIOGRAPHY

Bobby William Austin is Managing Director of the American Education Think Tank. Austin is the Writer/Editor of *Repairing the Breach*, cited by *Washington Post* columnist Bill Raspberry as," the plan to save America." He is Mahatma Gandhi Fellow of the American Academy of Political and Social Science.